A Prairie Home Companion®

PRETTY GOOD JOKE BOOK

NEW 3RD EDITION

HIGHBRIDGE COMPANY
MINNEAPOLIS, MINNESOTA

Published by
HighBridge Company
33 S Sixth St, CC-2205
Minneapolis, MN 55402

2   3   4   5   6   7   8   9   10

Joke research by Brian Becker, Joyce Besch, Melissa Christensen, Mike
Danforth, Alan Frechtman, Kay Gornick, Kate Gustafson, Tiffany Hanssen,
Kathryn Hauser, Rob Knowles, Laura Levine, Kathy Mack, Andrea Murray,
David O'Neill, Katy Reckdahl, Hillary Rhodes, Russ Ringsak, Elena See,
Vincent Voelz.

Graphic design by Christopher Marble
Printed in the United States of America

Library of Congress Cataloging-in-Publication Data

A Prairie home companion pretty good joke book.—New 3rd ed.
          p.   cm.
Joke research by Brian Becker...[et al.].
    ISBN 1-56511-804-9 (pbk.)
    1. American wit and humor. I. Becker, Brian. II. Prairie home
companion (Radio program)
    PN6165.P73   2003
    818'.60208—dc22

                                            2003015542

CONTENTS

INTRODUCTION

There are two ways to get to know people well in a short time, and one is to work alongside them at a hard and unpleasant job such as cleaning latrines or picking potatoes, and the other way is to tell jokes. Like the one about the grasshopper who comes into the bar and the bartender says, "Hey, we've got a drink named after you." And the grasshopper says, "Why would anyone name a drink Bob?" I've heard this joke a hundred times and it's still good. And the knock, knock joke about Sam and Janet Evening. And of course there's no plate like chrome for the hollandaise.

We only tell jokes now, we don't play them so much anymore. The golden age of practical jokes ended back before World War II, when cars could be taken apart and reassembled on a barn roof, when there were more farm animals who could be herded into somebody's bedroom, when many houses had an outhouse that could be tipped. But there's a big price to be paid for those jokes: nobody wants to be around you. Your father, that earnest and modest man, comes home and plops down in his easy chair with the newspaper and hears a blast from beneath the cushion, and he doesn't appreciate it. Nor does your mother when she drinks her orange juice and it dribbles down her blouse from the tiny holes in the joke glass you bought from the mail-order house. In olden times, there were men who spent weeks dreaming up gags to play on their friends, but they're dead now, and the people they played their jokes on are okay with that.

The Chatterbox Cafe in Lake Wobegon is a center of culture where gentlemen like to sit and tell jokes, and if you were new in town, you might come here to earn a little acceptance. If you sit on the periphery of a group of men telling jokes and you listen for a while and laugh appropriately and don't thrust yourself into the group but wait an appropriate length of time until there is a lull and then offer your joke and if it's a joke that is new to them and if you tell it well and don't flounder around in the setup, the crucial part of the joke, but tell it cleanly and simply with no missteps and not too much topspin, remembering this is Minnesota and we like it dry, no wheezing and chortling, and then you get to the elaboration where you can embroider a little and draw it out, if they're in the mood, and you do this gracefully, not overselling the joke, read your audience and just when they're ready for it you feed them the fat part, and then the punch line, and not laugh at the joke yourself until they do—then you'll be welcome here. Absolutely. No need to show a résumé or submit testimonials. If you can tell a joke, you're okay.

Jokes are democratic. Telling one right has nothing to do with having money or being educated. It's a knack, like hammering a nail straight. Anyone can learn it, and it's useful in all sorts of situations. You can go your whole life and not need math or physics for a minute, but the ability to tell a joke is always handy. Nobody knows where they come from. The week after the president admits that he did fool around with the intern, someone turns to you before a meeting and says, "They had a Presidents' Day Sale at Macy's and all men's pants were half off." Somebody must've come up with this, but it would slow

8

down the joke to put a byline on it and so it's told straight, no attribution. And within days, it flashes all over the country, by word of mouth and e-mail. Jokes are good for your health, they reduce stress, even ancient jokes like "She was only the stableman's daughter, but all the horsemen knew her," even jokes as old as "Does this bus go to Duluth? No, this bus goes beep beep." Or the blind man who picked up a hammer and saw. They keep on pleasing us, year after year.

At the Chatterbox, you never, never sit around and talk about humor. You don't say, "I don't know why, I just can't remember jokes," or "People sure don't tell as many jokes as they used to, do they," you simply sit in your chair and drink your coffee and the conversation hops around in a surrealistic way from hunting to dogs and cats, and then to elephants and Alzheimer's and old age, sex, Lutherans, and you lean back and say, "I read in the paper the other day that the nursing homes are giving out Viagra." And someone says, "Oh really?" And you say, "Yeah, they're starting to give it to the old guys to keep 'em from rolling out of bed." Your clothes may be disheveled and your life in chaos, you may be of the wrong race or religion, but if you can tell a joke well, you'll be accepted.

—GARRISON KEILLOR

ONE-LINERS

A clear conscience is the sign of a bad memory.

For every action, there is an equal and opposite criticism.

He who hesitates is probably right.

Depression is merely anger without enthusiasm.

Eagles may soar, but weasels don't get sucked into jet engines.

I went to buy some camouflage clothing, but I couldn't find it.

My wife went to a self-help group for compulsive talkers. It's called On & On Anon.

"Veni, Vidi, Velcro"—I came, I saw, I stuck around.

I'm reading a terrifically interesting book about anti-gravity—I just can't put it down.

I always wanted to be somebody, but I guess I should have been more specific.

If you are what you eat, I'm dead meat.

Middle age is having a choice of two temptations and choosing the one that will get you home earlier.

Seen it all, done it all, can't remember most of it.

It's a cruel choice: work or daytime television.

Lead me not into temptation—I can find the way myself.

The sooner you fall behind, the more time you'll have to catch up.

I intend to live forever—so far, so good.

I have seen the truth and it makes no sense.

The best part about owning a restaurant for cats is that your customers don't complain when they get hair in their food.

The best part about fighting your way to the top of the food chain is that you can choose to be a vegetarian or not.

The best part about computers is that they make very fast, accurate mistakes.

My software never has bugs—it just develops random features.

According to my calculations the problem doesn't exist.

A Freudian slip is when you say one thing but you mean your mother.

Everyone has a photographic memory. Some people are just out of film.

Just when I was getting used to yesterday, along came today.

Sometimes I think I understand everything—then I regain consciousness.

Save the whales! Trade them for valuable prizes.

I said no to drugs, but they just wouldn't listen.

Age doesn't always bring wisdom. Sometimes age comes alone.

A bus station is where a bus stops. A train station is where a train stops. Now you know why they call it a workstation.

The difference between capitalism and communism is that under communism man exploits man, whereas under capitalism it's the other way around.

My pig learned karate. Now he's doing pork chops.

I'd rather have this bottle in front of me than a frontal lobotomy.

Politicians and diapers should both be changed regularly—and for the same reason.

God grant me the senility to forget the people I never liked, the good fortune to run into the ones I do, and the eyesight to tell the difference.

OLD STANDBYS

Someday we'll look back on all this and plow into
a parked car.

Everybody is somebody else's weirdo.

Alcohol and calculus don't mix. Never drink and derive.

Don't sweat the petty things and don't pet the sweaty
things.

If at first you don't succeed, skydiving is definitely not
for you.

Some days you're the dog, some days you're the hydrant.

Some days you're the bug, some days you're the windshield.

Health is merely the slowest possible rate at which one
can die.

It's not the pace of life that concerns me, it's the sudden
stop at the end.

Those who live by the sword get shot by those who don't.

The only reason I'd take up jogging is so I could hear heavy
breathing again.

Sometimes I feel like a man trapped in a woman's body.
　　But luckily that man is gay, so nobody seems to notice.

If you're going to try cross-country skiing, start with a small country.

Never say anything bad about a man until you've walked a mile in his shoes. By then he's a mile away, you've got his shoes, and you can say whatever you want to.

Time may be a great healer, but it's a lousy beautician.

The early bird gets the worm, but it's the second mouse who gets the cheese.

When I'm not in my right mind, my left mind gets pretty crowded.

Why is it called a building when it has already been built?

He is not quiet; he is a conversational minimalist.

He was the number one laxative salesman in the whole United States, but he was just a regular guy.

He does not have a beer belly; he has developed a liquid grain-storage facility.

He does not get lost; he discovers alternative destinations.

He is not short and wide; he is anatomically compact.

He does not eat like a pig; he suffers from reverse bulimia.

Twenty-four hours in a day, twenty-four beers in a case. Coincidence?

Do Roman nurses refer to IVs as 4s?

Why is the alphabet in that order? Is it because of the song?

Have you ever imagined a world with no hypothetical situations?

You go to the ballet and you see girls dancing on their tiptoes. Why don't they just get taller girls?

If corn oil comes from corn, where does baby oil come from?

Why is "abbreviation" such a long word?

What's another word for "thesaurus"?

Do they sterilize the needles for lethal injections?

Why isn't "phonetic" spelled the way it sounds?

If a cow laughed, would milk come out of her nose?

Why do they put braille dots on the keypad of the drive-up ATM?

Why is "brassiere" singular and "panties" plural?

If you ate pasta and antipasta, would you still be hungry?

If the black box survives a plane crash, why isn't the whole airplane made out of the stuff?

Why do they report power outages on TV?

Why is it called tourist season if we can't shoot them?

Is there another word for "synonym"?

Why is there an expiration date on sour cream?

Why are builders afraid to have a 13th floor, but book publishers aren't afraid to have a Chapter 11?

Shouldn't there be a shorter word for "monosyllabic"?

If we aren't supposed to eat animals, why are they made of meat?

As you grow older, do you miss the innocence and idealism of your youth, or do you mostly miss cherry bombs?

Did you know that half of all people are below average?

Lawyers get disbarred and clergymen defrocked. So doesn't it make sense that ballplayers would be debased, politicians devoted, and cowboys deranged, models deposed, Calvin Klein models debriefed, organ donors delivered, and dry cleaners depressed, decreased, and depleted?

17

Birth-control pills are tax deductible, but only if they don't work.

What do you get when you use LSD along with birth control pills?
A trip without the kids.

What's the birth rate in your town?
Same as everywhere: one per person.

Why is it great to be a test tube baby?
You get a womb with a view.

Lady, this vacuum cleaner will cut your work in half.
Good. I'll take two of them.

Two goldfish are in a tank and one says to the other, "Do you know how to drive this thing?"

Did you hear that Ford announced a huge recall of late-model Mercurys?
They found traces of tuna in them.

What's the difference between beer nuts and deer nuts?
Beer nuts are $1.69 and deer nuts are under a buck.

What did the doe say when she came out of the woods?
Boy, I'll never do that again for two bucks.

Did you hear about the blind man who picked up a hammer and saw?

A man walks up to a blind man and hands him a piece of matzo. The blind man says, "Who wrote this nonsense?"

What is the difference between ignorance, apathy, and ambivalence?
  I don't know and I don't care one way or the other.

If you could have a conversation with someone, living or dead, who would it be?
  I'd choose the one who's living.

Did you hear Willie Nelson got hit by a car?
  He was playing on the road again.

Did you hear about the invisible man who married the invisible woman?
  Yeah, their kids aren't much to look at either.

Excuse me, does this bus go to Duluth?
  No, this bus goes beep beep.

How do they circumcise a whale?
  They send down four skin divers.

Did you hear about the dyslexic devil worshipper?
  He sold his soul to Santa.

What do the letters DNA stand for?
  National Dyslexics' Association.

When it comes right down to it, dyslexics have more nuf.

Why not say "288" in polite conversation?
    Because it's two gross.

What did the fish say when he hit a concrete wall?
    Dam.

Did you hear about the home brewer who entered his first brewing contest?
    The report he got back read: "Dear Sir, your horse has diabetes."

If H_2O is on the inside of a fire hydrant, what is on the outside?
    K_9P.

Did you hear that in New York the Stop and Shop grocery chain merged with the A&P?
    Now it's called the Stop&P.

Did you hear about the new restaurant that opened in India?
    It's a New Delhicatessen.

How do you get an elephant out of the theater?
    You can't. It's in their blood.

What's big and gray and wrote gloomy poetry?
    T. S. Elephant.

PUNS

There once were identical twins—born in Greece and separated at birth—put up for adoption. One was sent off to Saudi Arabia, and he was named Amal. The other one was sent off to Spain, and he was named Juan. Many years later, their relatives arranged for a reunion. It was a big event, and everyone showed up at the airport in Greece to greet the twins. The plane from Spain landed, and off came Juan, to the delight of the crowd. Then they waited for the plane from Saudi Arabia. Soon it arrived, but Amal wasn't on it—he'd missed the plane. One relative said to the other, "Well, they are identical twins. And if you've seen Juan, you've seen Amal."

A young snail decided that he wanted to buy himself a sporty car with all the amenities.

He went into a dealership that specialized in sports cars and selected one with everything he had always wanted.

As the salesman was finishing the special order form, the snail said, "There's one thing more. I want a large letter S on each side of the car."

The salesman said, "We can do that with no problem. Would you mind telling me why?"

The snail replied, "No, not at all. When I drive down the street I want to hear people say, 'Look at that little S car go!'"

I would like to go to Holland someday. Wooden Shoe?

Leif Erickson returned home from a voyage and found his name missing from the town register. His wife insisted on complaining to the local civic official, who apologized profusely, saying, "I'm sorry, Mrs. Erickson, I must have taken Leif off my census."

A farmer is milking his cow and as he is milking, a fly comes along and flies into the cow's ear. A little bit later, the farmer notices the fly in the milk. The farmer says, "Hmph. In one ear, out the udder."

So, these vultures decided to fly to Florida on an airline. They got on board carrying six dead raccoons, and the flight attendant said, "I'm sorry, but there's a limit of two carrion per passenger."

What do you call the cabs lined up at the Dallas airport?
    The yellow rows of taxis.

This duck walks into a drugstore and he says, "Gimme some Chapstick and put it on my bill."

Did you hear that NASA has launched several holsteins into low earth orbit?
    It was the herd shot around the world.

Did you hear about the frog who wanted to get out of the construction business, but sadly, all he could do was rivet, rivet, rivet...

"I was in Mercy, Australia, and I was served tea made from the hair of a koala."

"Made from the hair of a koala? You're kidding! How was it?"

"Oh, it was awful. It was filled with koala hair!"

"Well, you know, the koala tea of Mercy is not strained."

This doctor always got really stressed out at work. So every day on his way home, he'd stop and see his friend Dick, the bartender. Dick would know the doctor was coming, and he'd have an almond daiquiri ready for him. The doctor would come in and have his almond daiquiri and go home. One day Dick ran out of almonds, and he thought, "Well, the doctor won't know the difference." So he cut up this hickory nut and made a daiquiri with it. When the doctor came by, Dick put the drink in front of him. The doctor took a sip and said, "Is this an almond daiquiri, Dick?" And Dick said, "No, it's a hickory daiquiri, Doc."

There's a nudist colony for communists. Two old men are sitting on the front porch. One turns to the other and says, "I say, old boy, have you read Marx?" And the other says, "Yes…I believe it's these wicker chairs."

23

Recently, a Frenchman in Paris nearly got away with stealing several paintings from the Louvre. However, after planning the crime and getting in and out and past security, he was captured only two blocks away when his Econoline ran out of gas. When asked how he could mastermind such a crime and then make such an obvious error, he replied, "I had no Monet to buy Degas to make the Van Gogh."

Early one spring morning, Papa Mole decided to check out the sounds and smells of the new season. He traveled along his burrow until he could stick his head out and survey the area. It was such a beautiful morning, he quickly called to Mama Mole to come join him. Papa Mole said, "It is such a beautiful spring morning. I hear the birds singing and I smell…bacon…yes, someone is frying! It smells so good." Mama Mole said, "It is indeed a beautiful morning and…why, yes…I think I smell someone cooking pancakes. Yes, delicious buckwheat pancakes! Come quick, Baby Mole, you must experience these delectable sounds and smells!" Baby Mole raced along the burrow but could not squeeze past his parents. Mama said, "Do you smell those delicious smells of breakfast, Baby Mole? Doesn't it make you hungry and happy that spring is here?" Baby Mole replied, somewhat disgruntled, his voice a bit muffled as he tried to squeeze past his parents again, "I wouldn't know. All I can smell is molasses!"

Out in the Pacific Ocean, Sam and his wife Sue, two clams, owned a restaurant that had live disco music every Saturday night. Their diner was known for its great musicians, the shrimp quartet. Bob played guitar, Chuck played the drums, Sally sang, and Harry played the harp. One day while crossing the street, Harry the shrimp was involved in an accident and was trampled to death by an urchin driving an out-of-control sea horse. Everyone at Sam's disco was devastated. Without old Harry playing his harp, the disco just wouldn't be the same. Even Harry, now in heaven, was sad. He asked St. Peter if he could go back just once more and play with the shrimp quartet on a hopping Saturday disco night. St. Peter said yes and allowed him to leave heaven for one night. Harry joined the shrimp in their disco frenzy and had a great time catching up with all his old crustacean friends. When the night was over, he sadly returned to heaven. St. Peter looked at him and asked, "Harry, where is your harp?" Harry sighed, "I guess," he paused, "I left my harp in Sam Clam's disco."

Mahatma Gandhi walked barefoot everywhere, to the point that the soles of his feet became quite thick and hard. Being a very spiritual person, he ate very little and often fasted. As a result, he was quite thin and frail. Furthermore, due to his diet, he ended up with very bad breath. Therefore, he came to be known as a super callused, fragile mystic plagued with halitosis.

Two boll weevils grew up in South Carolina. One went to Hollywood and became a famous actor. The other stayed behind in the cotton fields and never amounted to much. The second one naturally became known as the lesser of two weevils.

An elephant and a giraffe come down to the watering hole for a drink. They see a turtle fast asleep, basking in the sun. The elephant goes over and kicks the turtle—wack—to the other shore. "Boy, that was cruel," said the giraffe. "Why did you do that?" The elephant said, "That turtle bit a big chunk out of my trunk fifty years ago." "Fifty years ago! Wow, what a great memory," said the giraffe. "Yes," said the elephant, "I have turtle recall."

This guy goes into a restaurant for a Christmas breakfast while in his hometown for the holidays. After looking over the menu he says, "I'll just have the eggs Benedict." His order comes a while later, and it's served on a big, shiny hubcap. He asks the waiter, "What's with the hubcap?"

The waiter sings, "O, there's no plate like chrome for the hollandaise!"

There was a horse trainer who raised a filly, and when he raced her in the evening she always won, but when she raced during the day she lost.

She was a fine horse, but she was a real night mare.

A man who lived in a block of apartments thought it was raining and put his hand out the window to check. Just as he did this, a glass eye fell into his hand. He looked up to see where it came from and saw a young woman looking down from an upstairs window.

"Is this yours?" he asked.

She said, "Yes, could you bring it up?"

When he got up to her apartment, he found she was extremely attractive, and she offered him a drink. After they'd finished their drinks, she said, "I'm about to have dinner. There's plenty; would you like to join me?"

He readily accepted her offer, and they both enjoyed a lovely meal. After dinner, she said, "I've had a marvelous evening. Would you...like to stay the night?"

The man hesitated, then said, "Wow, do you act like this with every man you meet?"

"No," she replied, "only those who catch my eye."

Did you hear about the fire at a Basque movie theater? Unfortunately there was only a single emergency exit door, so several people were trampled.

Which only goes to show that you shouldn't put all your Basques in one exit.

Did you hear that Miss Muffet and Saddam Hussein got together for a meeting last week to discuss their common problem?

They both have Kurds in their way.

A group of chess enthusiasts checked into a hotel and were standing in the lobby discussing their recent tournament victories. After about an hour the manager came out of the office and asked them to disperse. "But why?" they asked, as they moved off. "Because," he said, "I can't stand chess nuts boasting in an open foyer."

One day, a Russian couple was walking down the street, and they got into an argument over whether it was raining or sleeting. So they asked a communist party official, Comrade Rudolph, if it was officially raining or sleeting. "Today it is officially raining, Comrades," said the official, and walked away. The wife said, "I still think it's sleeting." The man said, "Rudolph the Red knows rain, dear."

Darth Vader: "Luke Skywalker, I know what you're getting for Christmas."

Luke: "How do you know?"

Vader: "I felt your presents."

What is the difference between a joist and a girder?

The first wrote "Ulysses," and the other wrote "Faust."

Did you hear about the Buddhist who refused novocaine during his root canal?

He wanted to transcend dental medication.

There was a man who entered a pun contest. He sent in ten different puns, in the hope that at least one of the puns would win. Unfortunately, no pun in ten did.

LIGHTBULB JOKES

How many procrastinators does it take to screw in a lightbulb?
   One, but he has to wait until the light is better.

How many women with PMS does it take to change a lightbulb?
   Six.
   Why?
   It just does, okay?

How many advertising execs does it take to change a lightbulb?
   Interesting question. What do you think?

How many art directors does it take to change a lightbulb?
   Does it have to be a lightbulb?

How many copy editors does it take to screw in a lightbulb?
   The last time this question was asked it involved art directors. Is the difference intentional? Should one or the other instance be changed? It seems inconsistent.

How many art students does it take to change a lightbulb?
   One, but he gets two credits.

How many grad students does it take to change a lightbulb?
   One, but it takes ten years.

How many University of Iowa freshmen does it take to screw in a lightbulb?

None. That's a sophomore course.

How many Yale students does it take to change a lightbulb?

None. New Haven looks better in the dark.

How many Minnesotans does it take to change a lightbulb?

Ten. One to change the bulb and 9 to apologize for it being out.

How many Californians does it take to change a lightbulb?

Six. One to turn the bulb, one for support, and four to relate to the experience.

How many narcissists does it take to change a lightbulb?

One. He holds the bulb while the world revolves around him.

How many existentialists does it take to screw in a lightbulb?

Two. One to screw it in, and one to observe how the lightbulb itself symbolizes a single incandescent beacon of subjective reality in a netherworld of endless absurdity reaching out toward a maudlin cosmos of nothingness.

How many Zen masters does it take to change a lightbulb?

Two. One to change it and one not to change it.

How many conservative economists does it take to change a lightbulb?

None. The darkness will cause the lightbulb to change by itself.

How many psychiatrists does it take to change a lightbulb?

One, but only if the lightbulb wants to change.

How many psychoanalysts does it take to screw in a lightbulb?

How long have you been having this fantasy?

How many surgeons does it take to change a lightbulb?

None. You don't need it out today, but if it continues to give you trouble in the future, you should consider removing it.

How many telemarketers does it take to change a lightbulb?

Only one, but she has to do it while you're eating dinner.

How many chiropractors does it take to change a lightbulb?

One, but it takes him three visits.

How many reference librarians does it take to screw in a lightbulb?

I don't know, I'll have to check on that and get back to you.

How many real estate agents does it take to change a lightbulb?

Ten, but we'll accept eight.

How many used car salesmen does it take to screw in a lightbulb?

I'm working out the figure on my calculator, and I think you'll be pleasantly surprised.

How many auto mechanics does it take to change a lightbulb?

We don't know yet, they're still waiting on a part.

How many statisticians does it take to change a lightbulb?

1.67.

How many IRS agents does it take to screw in a lightbulb?

Only one, but it really gets screwed.

How many real men does it take to change a lightbulb?

None. Real men aren't afraid of the dark.

How many lonely guys does it take to change a lightbulb?

One, but he wishes it was two.

How many dull people does it take to change a lightbulb?

One.

How many football players does it take to change a lightbulb?

The entire team! And they all get a semester's credit for it.

How many Irishmen does it take to change a lightbulb?

Fifteen. One to hold the bulb and the rest to drink whiskey until the room spins.

How many brewers does it take to change a lightbulb?

About one third less than for a regular bulb.

How many pro-lifers does it take to change a lightbulb?

Six. Two to screw in the bulb and four to testify that it was lit from the moment they began screwing.

How many data base people does it take to change a lightbulb?

Three: One to write the lightbulb removal program, one to write the lightbulb insertion program, and one to act as a lightbulb administrator to make sure nobody else tries to change the lightbulb at the same time.

How many internet mail list subscribers does it take to change a lightbulb?

155. One to change the lightbulb and to post to the mail list that the lightbulb has been changed, 11 to share similar experiences of changing lightbulbs, 109 to post that this list is not about lightbulbs, 27 to post URLs where one can see examples of different lightbulbs, three to post about links they found from the URLs that are relevant to this list, and four to suggest that posters read the lightbulb FAQ.

How many tech guys does it take to change a lightbulb?

We have received your request concerning your hardware problem, and have assigned your request Service Number 39712. Please use this number for any future reference to this lightbulb issue. As soon as a technician becomes available, you will be contacted.

How many software developers does it take to change a lightbulb?

None. The lightbulbs are working fine in all the other offices, so yours must be all right, too.

How many programmers does it take to change a lightbulb?

None. That's a hardware problem.

How many Microsoft technicians does it take to change a lightbulb?

Three. Two to hold the ladder, and one to screw the lightbulb into a faucet.

How many IBM engineers does it take to change a burnt-out lightbulb?

None. They merely change the standard to darkness and upgrade the customers.

How many IBM PC owners does it take to screw in a lightbulb?

Only one, but he'll have to go out and buy the lightbulb adapter card first, which is extra.

How many accountants does it take to screw in a lightbulb?
What kind of answer did you have in mind?

How many doctors does it take to change a lightbulb?
What kind of insurance do you have?

How many Lutherans does it take to change a lightbulb?
Five. One to screw in the new bulb and four to talk about how much they'll miss the old one.

How many Amish does it take to change a lightbulb?
What's a lightbulb?

What do Catholics say when they change a lightbulb?
Glory be unto the Father and unto the Son and into the hole he goes.

How many charismatic Pentecostals does it take to change a lightbulb?
Hard to tell. All their hands are in the air already.

How many Unitarians does it take to change a lightbulb?
We believe that incandescent, fluorescent, tinted, or three-way are equally valid paths to light, and if, in your journey, you have felt the need to change your lightbulb, we are holding a lightbulb service on Sunday at which you're welcome to recite a poem or perform a dance about luminescence.

How many Christian Scientists does it take to screw in a lightbulb?

One. He prays for the old bulb to come back on.

How many dyslexics does it take to change a lightbulb?

Two. One to ladder the hold, the other to bulb in the screw.

How many surrealists does it take to change a lightbulb?

To get to the other side.

How many surrealists does it take to screw in a lightbulb?

Two. One to hold the giraffe and one to put the clocks in the bathtub.

How many performance artists does it take to change a lightbulb?

I don't know, I left at intermission.

How many sopranos does it take to change a lightbulb?

• Two. One to hold the diet cola and the other to get her accompanist to do it.

• Four. One to change the bulb and three to pull the chair out from under her.

How many French horn players does it take to change a lightbulb?

Just one, but he'll spend two hours checking it to make sure it doesn't leak.

How many lead guitarists does it take to change a lightbulb?

None—they just steal somebody else's light.

How many drummers does it take to change a lightbulb?

Just one, so long as the roadie gets the ladder, sets it up and puts the bulb in the socket for him.

How many drummers does it take to change a lightbulb?

None: they have a machine to do that now.

How many sound men does it take to change a lightbulb?

One. Upon finding no replacement, he takes the original apart, repairs it with a chewing gum wrapper and duct tape, changes the screw mount to bayonet mount, finds an appropriate patch cable, and re-installs the bulb fifty feet from where it should have been, to the satisfaction of the rest of the band.

How many singers does it take to screw in a lightbulb?

Eighteen. One to do it, and seventeen to be on the guest list.

How many bluegrass musicians does it take to change a lightbulb?

Four. One to change it and three to complain that it's electric.

How many jazz musicians does it take to change a lightbulb?

Don't worry about the changes. We'll fake it!

How many Deadheads does it take to change a lightbulb?
One to change it, 2,000 to take pictures of it, and 10,000 to follow it around until it burns out.

How many punk rockers does it take to change a lightbulb?
Two. One to change it and the other to eat the old one.

How many skateboarders does it take to change a lightbulb?
One, dude.

How many communists does it take to screw in a lightbulb?
The lightbulb contains the seeds of its own revolution.

How many Republicans does it take to change a lightbulb?
Twelve to investigate Clinton's involvement in the failure of the old bulb, 23 to deregulate the lightbulb industry and 51 to pass a tax credit for lightbulb changes.

How many Republicans does it take to change a lightbulb?
Two. One to mix the martinis and one to call the electrician.

How many Democrats does it take to change a lightbulb?
One to change the bulb, six to talk about how wonderful it's going to be when the new bulb is screwed in, and ten to argue for increased funding for solar lighting research.

How many liberals does it take to screw in a lightbulb?
Five. One to screw it in, and four to screw it up.

How many gay men does it take to screw in a lightbulb?

Two, but they would probably put in track lighting instead.

How many feminists does it take to change a lightbulb?

Sixteen. One to change it and fifteen to form a support group.

How many cockroaches does it take to change a lightbulb?

No one knows; when the light comes on they all scatter.

How many managers does it take to change a lightbulb?

None. They like to keep employees in the dark.

How many assistant managers does it take to change a lightbulb?

Three. Two to find out if it needs changing, and one to tell an employee to change it.

How many poets does it take to change a lightbulb?

Two. One to look at the bulb and think of his mother and one to stand at the window and watch the rain.

How many writers does it take to change a lightbulb?

Ten. One to change it and nine to say, "I could've done that."

How many Americans does it take to screw in a lightbulb in Afghanistan?

Only one, but he does it from 30 miles away using laser targeting.

How many monkeys does it take to change a lightbulb?
Two. One to screw it in, and one to scratch his butt.

How many directors does it take to change a lightbulb?
Three. No, make that four…on second thought three…well, better make it five, just to be safe.

How many matinee audience members does it take to change a lightbulb?
Two. One to do it and another to say, "Rose, he's changing the lightbulb."

How many public radio personalities does it take to change a lightbulb?
We'll have that answer right after this pledge break.

How many public radio people does it take to change a lightbulb?
Three. One to change the bulb, and two to do the pledging around it.

How many public radio hosts does it take to change a lightbulb?
Who needs lightbulbs? It's radio.

KNOCK, KNOCK JOKES

Knock, knock.
    Who's there?
    Frankfurter.
    Frankfurter who?
    Frankfurter lovely evening.

Knock, knock.
    Who's there?
    Dexter.
    Dexter who?
    Dexter halls with boughs of holly.

Knock, knock.
    Who's there?
    Fortification.
    Fortification who?
    Fortification, we're going to Miami.

Knock, knock.
    Who's there?
    Mr. Walter.
    Mr. Walter who?
    You don't Mr. Walter until the well runs dry.

Knock, knock.
  Who's there?
  Itzhak.
  Itzhak who?
  Itzhak sin to tell a lie.

Knock, knock.
  Who's there?
  Earl.
  Earl who?
  Earl-y bird gets the worm.

Knock, knock.
  Who's there?
  Amos.
  Amos who?
  Amos behavin'—savin' all my love for you.

Knock, knock.
  Who's there?
  Isabel.
  Isabel who?
  Isabel not working?

Knock, knock.
  Who's there?
  Carl.
  Carl who?
  Carl get you there faster than a bike.

Knock, knock.
  Who's there?
  Sam and Janet.
  Sam and Janet who?
  Sam and Janet Evening!

Knock, knock.
  Who's there?
  Fornication.
  Fornication who?
  Fornication like this you should wear a black tie.

Knock, knock.
  Who's there?
  Amarillo.
  Amarillo who?
  Amarillo-fashioned cowboy.

Knock, knock.
  Who's there?
  Euripides.
  Euripides who?
  Euripides pants, I breaka your face.

Knock, knock.
  Who's there?
  Justin.
  Justin who?
  Justin time for supper.

44

Knock, knock.
    Who's there?
    Diploma.
    Diploma who?
    Diploma is here to fix the sink.

Knock, Knock.
    Who's there?
    Ida.
    Ida who?
    Ida called first, but the phone's not working.

Knock, knock.
    Who's there?
    Knock, knock.
    Who's there?
    Knock, knock.
    Who's there?
    Knock, knock.
    Who's there?
    Knock, knock.
    Who's there?
    Philip Glass.

Knock, knock.
    Who's there?
    Repeat.
    Repeat who?
    Okay. Who, who, who, who, who.

Knock, knock.
  Who's there?
  Tarzan.
  Tarzan who?
  Tarzan Stripes Forever!

Knock, knock.
  Who's there?
  Debussy.
  Debussy who?
  Debussy Fields!

Knock, knock.
  Who's there?
  Wilbur Wright.
  Wilbur Wright who?
  Wilbur Wright back after this guitar solo!

Knock, knock.
  Who's there?
  Dewey.
  Dewey who?
  Dewey have to do these jokes all night?

Knock, knock.
  Who's there?
  Agatha.
  Agatha who?
  Agatha blues in the night!

Knock, knock.
    Who's there?
    Luke.
    Luke who?
    Luke for the silver lining…

Knock, knock.
    Who's there?
    Toreador.
    Toreador who?
    Open up or I'll toreador down!

Knock, knock.
    Who's there?
    Aardvark.
    Aardvark who?
    Aardvark a million miles for one of your smiles!

Knock, knock.
    Who's there?
    The German border patrol.
    The German border patrol who?
    Don't ask qvestions!

Knock, knock
    Who's there?
    Omelet.
    Omelet who?
    Omelet smarter than I look.

Knock, knock.
  Who's there?
  Panther.
  Panther who?
  Panther no panth, I'm going thwimming!

Knock, knock.
  Who's there?
  Bisquick!!
  Bisquick who?
  Bisquick!! Your pants are on fire.

Knock, knock.
  Who's there?
  Radio.
  Radio who?
  Radio not, here I come.

Knock, knock.
  Who's there?
  Eskimo Christians.
  Eskimo Christians who?
  Eskimo Christians, I tell you no lies.

Knock, knock.
  Who's there?
  Grace.
  Grace who?
  Grace skies are gonna clear up, put on a happy face.

Knock, knock.
  Who's there?
  Ammonia.
  Ammonia who?
  Ammonia bird in a gilded cage.

Knock, knock.
  Who's there?
  Olive.
  Olive who?
  Olive me, why not take olive me.

Knock, knock.
  Who's there?
  Ketchup.
  Ketchup who?
  Ketchup falling star and put it in your pocket....

Knock, knock.
  Who's there?
  Osbourne.
  Osbourne who?
  Osbourne under a bad sign.

Knock, knock.
  Who's there?
  Alex.
  Alex who?
  Alexplain it later.

Knock, knock.
  Who's there?
  Charlotta.
  Charlotta who?
  Charlotta bad jokes around here!

Knock, knock.
  Who's there?
  Saul.
  Saul who?
  Saul there is; there ain't no more.

CHICKEN JOKES

A chicken goes into the library, walks up to the librarian, and says, "Book."

The librarian says, "You want a book?"

"Book."

"Any book?"

"Book."

So the librarian gives the chicken a novel and off it goes. An hour later the chicken comes back and says, "Book-book."

The librarian says, "Now you want two books?"

"Book-book."

So she gives the chicken two more novels. The chicken leaves but again comes back later.

"Book-book-book."

"Three books?"

"Book-book-book."

So the librarian gives the chicken three books, but she decides she'll follow the chicken and find out what's going on. And the chicken goes down the alley, out of town and toward the woods, into the woods and down to the river, down to the swamp, and there is a bullfrog. The chicken sets the books down by him. The bullfrog looks at the books and says, "Reddit…Reddit…Reddit…"

Ham and eggs: a day's work for a chicken, a lifetime commitment for a pig.

A man walks into a restaurant and says, "How do you prepare your chickens?"

The cook says, "Nothing special. We just tell 'em they're gonna die."

What did the chick say when it saw an orange in the nest?
Look at the orange mama laid.

How do baby hens dance the tango?
They dance it chick to chick.

Why do hens lay eggs?
If they dropped them, they'd break.

Why do chicken coops have two doors?
Because if they had four, they'd be chicken sedans.

One day a traveling salesman was driving down a country road when he was passed by a three-legged chicken. He stepped on the gas, but at fifty miles per hour the chicken was still ahead. After a few miles, the chicken ran up a driveway and into a barn behind an old farmhouse.

The salesman drove up to the house and knocked at the door. When he told the farmer what he'd just seen, the farmer said that his son was a geneticist and had developed this breed of chicken so that he, his wife, and his son could each get a drumstick. The salesman said, "That's fantastic. How do they taste?" The farmer said, "I don't know. We can't catch 'em."

The chicken and the egg are lying in bed. The chicken is smiling and smoking a cigarette, but the egg is upset. She mutters to herself, "Well, I guess we answered that question."

Why did the fried chicken cross the road?
    She saw a fork up ahead.

Why did the turkey cross the road?
    It was the chicken's day off.

Why did the chicken cross the road?
    To get to the other side.

Why did the egg cross the road?
    It had an inclination.

Why did the baby cross the road?
    It was stapled to the chicken.

How cold was it?
    It was so cold I saw a chicken with a capon.

How windy was it?
    It was so windy that the chicken turned her back to the wind and laid the same egg six times.

Why did the chicken cross the road?

The New York City policeman said, "You give me five minutes with the chicken and I'll find out."

The Bible says, "And God said unto the chicken, 'Thou shalt cross the road.' And the chicken crossed the road, and there was much rejoicing."

Hemingway said, "He crossed the road. To die. In the rain."

Martin Luther King Jr. said, "I see a world where all chickens will be free to cross roads and no one will ask why."

Einstein said, "Did the chicken cross the road or was the road moved to the other side of the chicken?"

The President said, "To the best of my recollection, that chicken did not engage in what I would call road-crossing behavior."

THIRD GRADER JOKES

Why were all the ink spots crying?
　　Their father was in the pen.

Why did the mushroom go to the party?
　　Cuz he was a fungi!
Why did the fungi leave the party?
　　Cuz there wasn't mushroom!

Why do they put bells on cows?
　　Because their horns don't work.

Why did the scientist install a knocker on his door?
　　To win the no-bell prize.

What's brown and lives in the bell tower?
　　The lunch bag of Notre Dame.

What's brown and sounds like a bell?
　　Dung!

What's brown and sticky?
　　A stick.

What do you call a boomerang that doesn't work?
　　A stick.

Why are there so many Johnsons in the phone book?
　　They all have phones.

Why do seagulls fly over the sea?
    Because if they flew over the bay, they'd be bagels.

How do you keep a bagel from getting away?
    Put lox on it!

What kind of bees give milk?
    Boobies.

What did the bee say to the flower?
    "Hey Bud, when do you open?"

What did Mrs. Bullet say to Mr. Bullet?
    We're going to have a beebee.

Why was the tomato red?
    Because it saw the salad dressing.

Hear about the ship that ran aground carrying a cargo of
red paint and black paint?
    The whole crew was marooned.

What lies at the bottom of the ocean and twitches?
    A nervous wreck!

Why is a giraffe's neck so long?
    Because its feet smell.

What's green and hangs from trees?
    Giraffe snot.

What's green and skates?
Peggy Phlegm.

What's green and slimy and marches through Europe killing people?
Snazis.

How do you get down from an elephant?
You don't get down from an elephant, you get down from a goose.

Why can't you have two elephants in your swimming pool at the same time?
Because they'd only have one pair of trunks.

What should you do if you're eaten by an elephant?
Run around and around till you're all pooped out.

Why is an elephant big, gray, and wrinkled?
Because if he was small, white, and round he'd be an aspirin.

What do you get when you cross a fly with an elephant?
A zipper that never forgets.

How do you make an elephant fly?
First, you start with a 48-inch zipper...

Can an elephant jump higher than a lamppost?
Yes. Lampposts can't jump.

Why do elephants paint their toenails red?
  So they can hide in cherry trees.

What do you do with an elephant with three balls?
  Walk him and pitch to the rhino.

What's the worst part about hunting elephants?
  Carrying the decoys.

Why do elephants have trunks?
  Because they would look silly with glove compartments.

What is large, gray, and wears glass slippers?
  Cinderelephant.

Why was Cinderella so lousy at baseball?
  She ran away from the ball, and she had a pumpkin for a coach.

Why should you never fly with Peter Pan?
  Because you'll never, never land.

Why did the banker break up with his girlfriend?
  He lost interest.

Why did the Indian have a hard time getting into the hotel?
  He didn't have a reservation.

Why did the atoms cross the road?
  It was time to split!

Why was the baby ant so confused?
    Because all his uncles were ants.

Why did Humpty Dumpty have a great fall?
    He wanted to make up for a lousy summer.

Where did the king keep his little armies?
    Up his little sleevies.

Did you hear about the corduroy pillows?
    They're making headlines, aren't they?

What is the last thing that goes through a bug's mind as it
hits a windshield?
    His butt.

Why do gorillas have large nostrils?
    Because they have big fingers.

Dad, I'm going to a party. Would you do my homework
for me?
    I'm sorry, kid, but it just wouldn't be right.
    Well, maybe not. Give it a try anyway.

Where do otters come from?
    Otter Space.

How does the man on the moon get his hair cut?
    Eclipse it.

Did you hear about the restaurant on the moon?
    The food is terrific, but there's no atmosphere.

Why is a moon rock tastier than an earth rock?
  Because it's a little meteor.

What did the number 0 say to the number 8?
  Nice belt!

Why was the math book sad?
  Because it had so many problems.

Why did the cookie visit the doctor?
  He felt crummy.

What did the hot dog say when he crossed the finish line?
  I'm the wiener!

What did one hot dog say to another?
  Hi, Frank.

Why do hummingbirds hum?
  Because they can't remember the words.

What is bright orange and sounds like a parrot?
  A carrot.

Why do birds fly south for the winter?
  Because it's too far to walk.

Did you hear about the skunk who went to church?
  He had his own pew.

Why couldn't the pony talk?
    He was a little horse.

What has four legs and one arm?
    A Rottweiler.

What do you get when you cross a pit bull with a collie?
    A dog that rips your leg off, then goes for help.

What do you get when you cross a cantaloupe with a
Border collie?
    Melancholy babies.

What does a dog do that a man steps into?
    Pants.

What do you call a dog that is left-handed?
    A southpaw.

Where do you find a no-legged dog?
    Right where you left him.

Whatdaya call a dog with no legs?
    Don't matter, he ain't gonna come anyway.

So the male flea said to the female flea, "How about we go
to the movies?"
    And the female flea said, "Sure. Shall we walk or take
the dog?"

Bert asked Ernie if he wanted ice cream, and Ernie said, "Sure, Bert."

Did you hear about the snail that got beat up by two turtles?

He went to the police and they asked him, "Did you get a good look at the turtles who did this?"

He said, "No, it all happened so fast."

Did you hear about the two silkworms in a race?

They wound up in a tie.

Who yelled, "Coming are the British"?

Paul Reverse.

What did the mother buffalo say to her little boy when he went off to school?

Bison.

What's a metaphor?

So that livestock can graze.

What do you get when you eat onions and beans?

Tear gas.

Why did the man stop farting?

He ran out of gas.

What do you use to fix a broken tomato?

Tomato paste.

Why do golfers wear two pairs of pants?
    In case they get a hole in one.

What did the tie say to the hat?
    You go on a head, I'll just hang around.

Why didn't Noah fish very often?
    He only had two worms.

How much do pirates pay for their earrings?
    A buccaneer.

If Mr. and Mrs. Bigger had a baby, who would be the biggest of the three?
    The baby, because he's a little Bigger.

Did you hear about the two antennas that got married?
    The wedding was terrible, but the reception was great.

Where does a one-armed man shop?
    At a secondhand store!

What do you say to a hitchhiker with one leg?
    Hop in.

What did one ocean say to the other ocean?
    Nothing, they just waved.

What's a chimney sweep's most common ailment?
    The flue.

Where does satisfaction come from?
A satisfactory.

Why can't a woman ask her brother for help?
Because he can't be a brother and assist her too.

What do you get when you pour boiling water down a rabbit hole?
Hot cross bunnies.

Why did the bunnies go on strike?
They wanted a raise in celery.

What do you give a deer with an upset stomach?
Elkaseltzer.

What do you call a deer with no eyes?
No ideer.

How did the mouse feel after the cat chased it through a screen door?
Strained.

What do you call cheese that doesn't belong to you?
Nacho cheese.

What do Eskimos get from sitting on the ice too long?
Polaroids.

What do prisoners use to call each other?
Cell phones.

Why do bicycles fall over?
 Because they are two-tired.

What's Irish and sits outside?
 Patio Furniture.

What is Mary short for?
 She's just got little legs, I guess.

How do you fix a broken tuba?
 With a tuba glue.

Why did the composer only compose in bed?
 He was writing sheet music.

Why did the toilet paper roll down the hill?
 Because it wanted to get to the bottom.

What do Alexander the Great and Winnie the Pooh have in common?
 They have the same middle name.

What's the difference between roast beef and pea soup?
 Anyone can roast beef, but not many people can pee soup.

What do you call a guy who never farts in public?
 A private tooter.

Say lettuce and spell cup.
 Lettuce c-u-p.

65

A guy yells across the river, "Hey, how do you get to the other side of this river?"

A guy on the other side yells back, "You are on the other side!"

Did you hear about the giant that threw up?
No, how'd you know?
It's all over town.

What does a one-legged ballerina wear?
A one-one.

Why are you scratching yourself?
I'm the only one who knows where it itches.

Do you know how to make your own anti-freeze?
Take away her fur coat.

Why do fire departments have Dalmatians?
To help them find the hydrants.

Okay, class. If anyone has to go to the bathroom, just hold up two fingers.
How will that help?

INSULTS

I'd say he's about one Froot Loop shy of a full box.

The wheel's spinning, but the hamster's asleep.

I'd explain it to you but your brain would explode.

I like your approach...let's see your departure.

I'd say he doesn't have all his dogs on the same leash.

He forgot to pay his brain bill.

His antenna doesn't pick up all the channels.

I like you, but I don't want to see you working with subatomic particles.

Not the sharpest knife in the drawer, is he?

Doesn't have his belt through all the loops.

Where other people have a brain, he's got resonance.

Got an IQ that's about room temperature.

Got the IQ of garden tools.

Doesn't have the brainpower to toast a crouton.

He's so dense, light bends around him.

The gates are down, the lights are flashing, but the train just isn't coming.

I don't think his URL allows outside access.

A flash of light, a cloud of dust, and what was the question?

Looks like he played goalie for the darts team.

Definitely has a bad brains-to-testosterone ratio.

All booster, no payload.

I think he rode the Tilt-a-Whirl too long.

Hard to believe that he beat out a million other sperm.

He keeps a coat hanger in the backseat in case he locks the keys in his car.

I like long walks, especially when they're taken by people who annoy me.

Never underestimate the power of stupid people in large groups.

Here's a drum. Now beat it.

YO' MAMA JOKES

Yo' mama is so fat, she doesn't have a tailor, she has a contractor.

Yo' mama is so fat, she measures 36-24-36, and the other arm is just as big.

Yo' mama is so fat, she was in the Macy's Thanksgiving Day Parade…wearing ropes.

Yo' mama is so fat, she went on a light diet. As soon as it's light she starts eating.

Yo' mama is so fat, she's half Italian, half Irish, and half American.

Yo' mama is so fat, when her beeper goes off, people think she's backing up.

Yo' mama is so fat, when she goes to the movies, she sits next to everyone.

Yo' mama is so fat, when she goes in a restaurant she looks at the menu and says, "Okay…"

Yo' mama is so fat, she puts her lipstick on with a paint roller.

Yo' mama is so fat, she has to pull down her pants to get in her pocket.

TURN THE OTHER CHEEK

Yo' mama is so fat, you have to take a train and two buses just to get on her good side.

Yo' mama is so fat, she has to wake up in sections.

Yo' mama is so fat, she sat on a quarter and a booger popped out of George Washington's nose.

Yo' mama is so fat, she walked into the Gap and filled it.

Yo' mama is so fat, she has to put her belt on with a boomerang.

Yo' mama is so fat, she comes at you from all directions.

Yo' mama is so fat, when she was growing up she didn't play with dolls, she played with midgets.

Yo' mama is so fat, she uses two buses for roller-blades.

Yo' mama is so fat, when she goes to a buffet, she gets the group rate.

Yo' mama is so fat, she doesn't eat with a fork, she eats with a forklift.

Yo' mama is so fat, Weight Watchers won't look at her.

Yo' mama is so fat, the last time the landlord saw her, he doubled the rent.

Yo' mama is so fat, she put on some BVDs and by the time she got them on, they spelled "boulevard."

70

Yo' mama is so fat, I ran around her twice and got lost.

Yo' mama is so fat, the shadow of her butt weighs 100 pounds.

Yo' mama is so fat, the National Weather Service names each one of her farts.

Yo' mama is so fat, when she's standing on the corner police drive by and say, "Hey! Break it up!"

Yo' mama is so fat, she's been declared a natural habitat for condors.

Yo' mama is so fat, she sets off car alarms when she runs.

Yo' mama is so fat, when she goes to the zoo the elephants throw her peanuts.

Yo' mama is so fat, her blood type is Ragu.

Yo' mama is so fat, they had to let out the shower curtain.

Yo' mama is so fat that when she runs the fifty-yard dash she needs an overnight bag.

Yo' mama is so fat, she can't even fit in the chat room.

Yo' mama is so fat, she gets her toenails painted at Lucky's Auto Body.

Yo' mama is so fat, when she wears a yellow raincoat people holler, "Taxi!"

Yo' mama is so stupid, she stole a car and kept up the payments.

Yo' mama is so fat, when she gets in an elevator, it *has* to go down!

Yo' mama is so fat, she could sell shade.

Yo' mama is so fat, people jog around her for exercise.

Yo' mama is so fat, she gets runs in her jeans.

Yo' mama is so fat, when she wears a Malcolm X T-shirt, helicopters try to land on her back.

Yo' mama is so fat, she eats Wheat Thicks.

Yo' mama is so fat, she can't even jump to a conclusion.

Yo' mama is so fat that when she was born, she gave the hospital stretch marks.

Yo' mama is so fat, her graduation picture was an aerial photograph!

Yo' mama is so fat, her job title is spoon and fork operator!

Yo' mama is so fat, she left the house in high heels and when she came back, she had on flip-flops.

Yo' mama is so fat, when she turns around people throw her a welcome back party.

Yo' mama is so fat, her belly button doesn't have lint, it has sweaters.

Yo' mama is so fat, the last time she saw 90210 was on a scale.

Yo' mama is so fat, a picture of her would fall off the wall!

Yo' mama is so fat, when she gets on the scale, it says "To be continued."

Yo' mama is so fat, she sat on a dollar, and when she got up there were four quarters.

Yo' mama is so fat, she fell in love and broke it.

Yo' mama is so fat, when she takes a shower, her feet don't get wet!

Yo' mama is so fat, you have to grease the door frame and hold a Twinkie on the other side just to get her through.

Yo' mama is so fat, when she goes to an all-you-can-eat buffet, they have to install speed bumps.

TURN THE OTHER CHEEK

Yo' mama is so fat, the sign outside one restaurant says, "Maximum occupancy, 512, or Yo' mama!"

Yo' mama is so fat, she puts mayonnaise on aspirin.

Yo' mama is so fat, the back of her neck looks like a pack of hot dogs.

Yo' mama is so fat, her cereal bowl came with a lifeguard.

Yo' mama is so fat, she has to iron her pants on the driveway.

Yo' mama is so fat, when she goes to a restaurant, she doesn't get a menu, she gets an estimate.

Yo' mama is so fat, when she ran away, they had to use all four sides of the milk carton.

Yo' mama is so fat, she was zoned for commercial development.

Yo' mama is so fat, when she sings, it's over for everybody.

Yo' mama is so fat, she looks like she's smuggling a Volkswagen.

Yo' mama is so fat, when she was walking down the street and I swerved to miss her, I ran out of gas.

Yo' mama is so fat, when she dances, she makes the band skip.

Yo' mama is so fat, when she got her shoes shined, she had to take the guy's word for it.

Yo' mama is so fat, she gets group insurance!

Yo' mama is so fat, she's on both sides of the family!

Yo' mama is so fat, she can't reach her back pocket.

Yo' mama is so fat, she was born with a silver shovel in her mouth!

Yo' mama is so fat, when she fell over, she rocked herself to sleep trying to get up again.

Yo' mama is so fat, when she hauls ass, she has to make two trips!

Yo' mama is so fat, when she was diagnosed with a flesh-eating disease, the doctor gave her ten *years* to live!

Yo' mama is so fat, we're in her right now!

Yo' mama is so fat, when she sits around the house, she *sits around the house*!

Yo' mama is so fat, her bellybutton's got an echo!

Yo' mama is so fat, her bellybutton gets home fifteen minutes before she does!

Yo' mama is so fat, she had to go to Sea World to get baptized.

Yo' mama is so fat, when she tripped over on Fourth Avenue, she landed on Twelfth.

Yo' mama is so fat, she's got her own area code!

Yo' mama is so fat, when she talks to herself, it's a long distance call!

Yo' mama is so fat, she's got smaller fat women orbiting around her!

Yo' mama is so fat, whenever she goes to the beach, the tide comes in!

Yo' mama is so fat, she was born on the fourth, fifth, and sixth of March.

Yo' mama is so fat, she was floating in the ocean and Spain claimed her for the new world.

Yo' mama's so fat, she wears aluminum siding.

Yo' mama's so fat, she could fall down and wouldn't even know it.

Yo' mama's so fat, she got hit by a VW and had to go to the hospital to have it removed.

Yo' mama is so dumb, she thought Meow Mix was a record for cats.

Yo' mama is so dumb, she asked for a price check at the dollar store.

Yo' mama is so dumb, when she heard that 90 percent of all crimes occur in the home, she moved.

Yo' mama is so dumb, she called Dan Quayle for a spell check.

Yo' mama is so dumb, she thought that Tupac Shakur was a Jewish holiday.

Yo' mama's so dumb, she got locked in a grocery store and starved to death.

Yo' mama is so dumb, when she saw the sign that said, "Airport Left," she turned around and went home.

Yo' mama is so dumb, she thought Boyz II Men was a day-care center.

Yo' mama is so dumb, she sold the car for gas money.

TURN THE OTHER CHEEK

Yo' mama is so dumb, when she went to the movies and they said, "Under 17 not admitted," she went home and got sixteen friends.

Yo' mama is so dumb, when she missed the 44 bus, she took the 22 bus twice instead.

Yo' mama is so dumb, she went up on your roof because they said drinks were on the house!

Yo' mama is so dumb, she got fired from the M&M factory for throwing out the W's!

Yo' mama is so dumb, she only changed your diapers once a month because it said on the box "Good for up to 20 pounds"!

Yo' mama is so dumb, she thinks Johnny Cash is a pay toilet!

Yo' mama is so dumb, she sent me a fax with a stamp on it.

Yo' mama is so dumb, she bought a solar-powered flashlight.

Yo' mama is so dumb, she watches *The Three Stooges* and takes notes.

Yo' mama is so dumb, it took her two hours to watch *60 Minutes.*

Yo' mama is so dumb, she sits on the TV and watches the couch!

Yo' mama is so dumb, she stepped on a crack and broke her own back.

Yo' mama is so dumb, it takes her an hour to cook Minute Rice.

Yo' mama is so dumb, she cooked her own complimentary breakfast.

Yo' mama is so dumb, when your dad said it was chilly outside, she ran out with a spoon.

Yo' mama is so dumb, she sold the house to pay the mortgage!

Yo' mama is so dumb, she had to call the operator to get the number for 911!

Yo' mama is so dumb, they had to burn down the school to get her out of second grade.

Yo' mama is so dumb, when you stand next to her, you hear the ocean!

Yo' mama is so poor, she went to McDonald's and put a milk shake on layaway.

Yo' mama is so poor, she waves around a Popsicle and calls it air conditioning.

Yo' mama is so poor, when I saw her kicking a can down the street, I asked her what she was doing, and she said, "Moving."

Yo' mama is so poor, when she goes to Kentucky Fried Chicken, she has to lick other people's fingers!!

Yo' mama is so poor, when I ring the doorbell she says, "Ding!"

Yo' mama is so poor, they ask for her I.D. when she pays cash.

Yo' mama is so ugly, the psychiatrist makes her lie face down.

Yo' mama is so ugly, for Halloween she can trick-or-treat over the telephone!

Yo' mama is so ugly, if my dog looked like that, I'd shave his butt and walk him backwards.

Yo' mama is so ugly, your father takes her to work with him so he doesn't have to kiss her goodbye.

Yo' mama is so ugly, they're going to move Halloween to her birthday.

Yo' mama is so ugly, all her neighbors chipped in for curtains.

Yo' mama is so ugly, she makes onions cry.

Yo' mama is so ugly, she went to the beauty shop and it took three hours…for an estimate.

Yo' mama is so ugly, the Red Cross talked her out of being an organ donor.

Yo' mama is so ugly, when she was a baby, her incubator had tinted windows.

Yo' mama is so ugly, she'd scare a buzzard off a gut wagon.

Yo' mama is so ugly, she looks like she's been bobbing for french fries!

Yo' mama is so ugly, when she walks into a bank, they turn off the cameras.

Yo' mama is so ugly that when she sits on the beach, cats try to bury her.

Yo' mama's so ugly, when she entered an ugly contest, they said, "Sorry, no professionals."

Yo' mama is so ugly, she could scare the moss off a rock!

Yo' mama's so ugly, the only thing attracted to her is gravity.

Yo' mama is so ugly, when she looks in the mirror, the reflection ducks!

Yo' mama is so ugly, her face is closed on weekends!

Yo' mama is so ugly, when she was born, the doctor slapped your grandma!

Yo' mama is so ugly, they know what time she was born, because her face stopped all the clocks!

Yo' mama is so ugly, when she cries, the tears run up her face.

Yo' mama is so ugly, her mother had to feed her with a slingshot.

Yo' mama is so ugly, she could scare the chrome off a bumper!

Yo' mama is so ugly, when she talks, hairs fall out of my nose.

Yo' mama is so ugly, your father kisses her with a stuntman.

Yo' mama's so ugly, at her wedding everyone kissed the groom.

Yo' mama is so skinny, her eyes are single file.

Yo' mama is so skinny, her pajamas have only one stripe.

Yo' mama is so slow, her ancestors arrived on the June Flower.

Yo' mama is so old, she farts dust!

Yo' mama is so old, she walked into an antiques store and they kept her.

Yo' mama is so old, her driver's license has hieroglyphics on it!

Yo' mama is so old, she still owes Moses a quarter!

Yo' mama is so old, when she was young, rainbows were black and white!

Yo' mama is so old, when she was born, the Dead Sea was just getting sick!

Yo' mama is so old, she was a waitress at the Last Supper.

Yo' mama is so old, when she was in school, they didn't have history.

Yo' mama is so old, when I told her to act her own age, she died.

Yo' mama is so old, she has a picture of Moses in her yearbook.

Yo' mama is so old, her birth certificate says "expired" on it.

Yo' mama is so old, she knew Burger King when he was still a prince.

Yo' mama is so old, she sat behind Jesus in the third grade.

Yo' mama is so short, she poses for trophies!

Yo' mama is so short, when she pulls up her stockings, she can't see where she's going.

Yo' mama's so short, you can see her feet on her driver's license!

Yo' mama's arms are so short, she has to tilt her head to scratch her ear.

Yo' mama's head is so small, she got her ear pierced and died.

Yo' mama's nose is so big, you can go bowling with her boogers!

Yo' mama's lips are so big, Chap Stick had to invent a spray.

Yo' mama is so lazy, I've seen her step into a revolving door and wait.

Yo' mama's house is so dirty, roaches ride around on dune buggies!

Yo' mama's house is so dirty, she has to wipe her feet before she goes outside.

Yo' mama is so dirty, she brushes her teeth with chewing tobacco.

Yo' mama is so nasty, she joined the Four Horsemen: war, pestilence, death, famine, and yo' mama!

Yo' mama's underarms are so hairy, she looks like she has somebody in a headlock.

Yo' mama's armpits stink so bad, she made Right Guard turn left.

Yo' mama's teeth are so yellow, when she smiles, cars slow down.

Yo' mama is so cross-eyed, she dropped a dime and picked up two nickels.

Yo' mama's glasses are so thick, when she looks at a map she can see people waving.

Yo' mama is so cheap, when she takes out a dollar, George Washington blinks at the light.

Yo' mama is so tough, when carpenters buy a box of nails, they say, "Hand me some of those mamas."

DEATH/HEAVEN JOKES

A man went on vacation and arranged for his mother to stay at his house and take care of his cat. And, just to be sure, he asked his next-door neighbor if he would look in on them every day and make sure they were all right. "No problem," said the neighbor. The man flew off to Mexico and after a couple of days he called the neighbor and asked how things were going.

"Well," the neighbor said, "your cat died." "Geez," the guy said. "You have to come right out and tell me like that? Couldn't you have a little more consideration? I'm on vacation. Couldn't you have broken it to me a little more gently. Like first telling me that the cat was on the roof, then that the cat fell off the roof, then maybe the next day telling me you had taken the cat to the vet—like that, not *boom* all at once! By the way, how's my mom doing?"

"Well," said the neighbor, "she's up on the roof…"

Three friends die in a car accident, and they go to an orientation in heaven. They are all asked, "When you are in your casket and friends and family are mourning you, what would you like to hear them say about you?"

The first guy says, "I would like to hear them say that I was a great doctor in my time and a great family man."

The second guy says, "I would like to hear that I was a wonderful husband and a school teacher who made a huge difference in our children of tomorrow."

The last guy replies, "I would like to hear them say… '*Look, he's moving*'!!"

A woman dies and goes to heaven, and St. Peter takes her on a tour of heaven. They pass a pit where there are people gnashing their teeth and wailing, and the woman says, "Who's down there?"

St. Peter says, "Oh, those are the Catholics who ate meat on Fridays."

They walk a little farther and there is another pit with more groaning and wailing, and she says, "Okay, who's down there?"

St. Peter answers, "Those are the Baptists who went to dances."

And a little farther along, there is another pit and people down there gnashing their teeth and crying and ripping their garments, and she says, "And those people?"

And St. Peter says, "Those are the Episcopalians who ate their salads with their dessert forks."

"Madame fortune teller, tell me: Are there golf courses in heaven?"

"I have good news, and I have bad news."

"What's the good news?"

"The good news is that the golf courses in heaven are beautiful beyond anything you could imagine!"

"That's wonderful."

"And you'll be teeing off at 8:30 tomorrow morning."

"I see there's a funeral in town today."

"Yeah."

"Who died?"

"I'm not sure, but I think it's the one in the coffin."

Brett Favre and Randall Cunningham die and go to heaven. After Brett Favre enters the pearly gates, God takes him on a tour. He shows him a little two-bedroom house with a faded Packers banner hanging from the front porch and says, "This is your house, Brett. You know, most people don't get their own houses up here."

Favre looks at the house, then turns around and looks at the one sitting on top of the hill. It's a huge two-story mansion with Minnesota flags lining both sides of the sidewalk and a huge Vikings banner hanging between the marble columns.

Favre says, "Hey! How come I get this little two-bedroom house, and Randall Cunningham gets a huge mansion?"

God says, "That's not Cunningham's house, it's mine."

A husband and his wife were driving home one night and ran into a bridge abutment and both were killed. They arrived in heaven and found it was a beautiful golf course with a lovely clubhouse and fabulous greens. It was free and only for them, and the husband said, "You want to play a round?"

She said, "Sure." They teed off on the first hole, and she said, "What's wrong?"

He said, "You know, if it hadn't been for your stupid oat bran, we could have been here years ago."

Three souls appeared before St. Peter at the pearly gates. St. Peter asked the first one, "What was your last annual salary?" The soul replied, "$200,000; I was a trial lawyer." St. Peter asked the second one the same question. The soul answered, "$95,000; I was a realtor." St. Peter then asked the third soul the same question. The answer was "$8,000." St. Peter immediately said, "Cool! What instrument did you play?"

A minister dies and is waiting in line at the pearly gates. Ahead of him is a guy dressed in sunglasses, a loud shirt, a leather jacket, and jeans. St. Peter addresses this guy, "Who are you, so that I may know whether or not to admit you to the kingdom of heaven?"

The guy replies, "I am Joe Choen, taxi driver, of Las Vegas."

St. Peter consults his list. He smiles and says to the taxi driver, "Take this silken robe and golden staff and enter the kingdom of heaven." The taxi driver goes into heaven with his robe and staff, and it is the minister's turn.

He stands erect and booms out, "I am Joseph Snow, pastor of St. Mary's for the last forty-five years."

St. Peter consults his list. He says to the minister, "Take this cotton robe and wooden staff and enter the kingdom of heaven."

"Just a minute," says the minister. "That man was a taxi driver, and he gets a silken robe and golden staff. How can this be?"

"Up here, we work by results," says St. Peter. "While you preached, people slept; while he drove, people prayed."

A curious fellow died one day and found himself waiting in the long line of judgment. As he stood there he noticed that some souls were allowed to march right through the gates of heaven. Others were led over to Satan, who threw them into the burning pit. But every so often, instead of hurling a poor soul into the fire, Satan would toss a soul off to one side into a small pile.

After watching Satan do this several times, the fellow's curiosity got the best of him. So he strolled over and asked Satan, "Excuse me, prince of darkness. I'm waiting in line for judgment, and I couldn't help wondering why you're tossing those people aside instead of flinging them into the fires of hell with the others?"

"Ah, those," Satan said with a groan. "They're all from Seattle. They're too wet to burn yet."

This couple is killed the night before their wedding. They go to heaven, and they ask St. Peter if they can be married.

St. Peter says, "Okay. I'll come and get you when we can do that."

Ten years later, he tells the couple, "Okay. We can have your wedding now."

So they get married, and there's a minister and flowers and nice music and all, but pretty soon they realize they made a mistake.

They go to St. Peter and say they want a divorce. St. Peter says, "Okay. I'll come and tell you when we can do that."

The couple says, "How long will it take?"

And St. Peter says, "It took ten years to get a preacher up here. Who knows how long it's going to take before a lawyer shows up!"

Bill Gates died in a car accident. He found himself in purgatory being sized up by God. "Well, Bill, I'm going to let you decide where you want to go." Bill replied, "Well, thanks, God. What's the difference between the two?" God said, "I'm willing to let you visit both places briefly to help you make a decision." Bill said, "Okay, then, let's try hell first." So Bill went to hell. It was a beautiful, clean, sandy beach with clear waters. There were thousands of beautiful women running around, playing in the water, laughing and frolicking about. The sun was shining and the temperature was perfect. "This is great!" he told God. "If this is hell, I really want to see heaven!" "Fine," said God, and off they went.

Heaven was a high place in the clouds, with angels drifting about playing harps and singing. It was nice but not as enticing as hell. Bill thought for a moment and then said, "Hmm, I think I prefer hell." "Fine," replied God, "as you desire." So Bill Gates went to hell. Two weeks later, God decided to check up on him.

When God arrived in hell, he found Bill shackled to a wall, screaming amongst the hot flames in a dark cave. He was being burned and tortured by demons. "How's everything going, Bill?" God asked. Bill responded, his voice full of anguish and disappointment, "This is awful, this is not what I expected. I can't believe this happened. What happened to that other place with the beaches and the beautiful women playing in the water?" God says, "That was the screen saver."

Three nurses die and go up to heaven. And St. Peter says, "So, tell me—what did you do with your life?" The first nurse says, "Well, I worked in an emergency room, and it was really challenging. But we were able to help some people and I think that's worthwhile." St. Peter says, "That's fabulous—come on in. I hope you enjoy heaven."

And St. Peter turns to the second nurse and says, "So, what did you do with your life?" And the nurse says, "I worked in a hospice, and it was a little depressing, since everyone dies. But we were kind to people and I think that's worthwhile." St. Peter says, "That's great. Come on in—I hope you enjoy heaven."

Then he faces the remaining nurse and says, "So, what did you do with your life?" And the nurse says, "For the last years of my life, I worked as a managed-care nurse for an HMO." St. Peter wrinkles his brow and pulls out a calculator, a whole set of manuals, and a pencil. He spends time writing and scrunching up pieces of paper, and then looks up and says, "I can approve you for a five-day stay."

Man: Is this the mortuary? Listen. You better make arrangements for a funeral. My wife passed away.
Funeral director: What?! Your wife died two years ago.
Man: I got married again.
Funeral director: Oh! Congratulations!

A bunch of salesmen went to the funeral of another salesman. They looked down at him in his coffin.
"Gosh, he looks terrible. What did he have?"
"North Dakota, South Dakota, western Minnesota..."

A young woman saw a funeral procession going by. There was a black hearse, followed by an older woman leading a pit bull on a leash, and after that was another hearse, and behind that was a line of two hundred women walking single file. The young woman walked up to the older woman and said, "I'm sorry to intrude on your moment of grief, but I can't help asking, whose funeral is this?"

The woman said, "Well, my husband is in that hearse up there. The pit bull killed him when it discovered him with his girlfriend. She's in that hearse back there."

The young woman said, "Can I borrow that dog?"

The old woman replied, "Get in line."

So this guy dies and goes to heaven and St. Peter takes him down the hall past a number of doors and then St. Peter stops and says, "You have to be very very quiet going past that door. That's where the Mormons are and they think they're the only ones here."

This guy's father dies, and he tells the undertaker he wants to give his dad the very best. So they have the funeral, and the undertaker sends him a bill for $16,000. He pays it. A month later he gets a bill for $85, which he pays. The next month there's another $85 bill, and the next month there's another. Finally the guy calls up the undertaker. The undertaker says, "Well, you said you wanted the best for your dad, so I rented him a tux."

RELIGION JOKES

God was talking to one of his angels. He said, "Boy, I just figured out how to rotate Earth so it creates this really incredible twenty-four-hour period of alternating light and darkness." The angel said, "What are you going to do now?" God said, "Call it a day."

So Moses was talking with God, and Moses said, "Wait a minute. Let me get this straight. They get to keep the oil, and we cut off the tip of our what?"

Why is it dangerous to piss off a Unitarian?
    He might burn a question mark in your front lawn.

Why are Unitarians such bad singers?
    Because they're always reading ahead in the hymnal to see if they agree with it.

Did you hear about that new, liberal Episcopal church?
    It has six commandments and four suggestions.

What do you get when you cross a Lutheran and a Buddhist?
    Someone who sits up all night worrying about nothing.

What do you get when you cross a Unitarian with a Jehovah's Witness?
    Someone out knocking on doors for no apparent reason.

What's the difference between Baptists and Methodists?

Baptists won't wave to each other in the liquor store.

God calls up the Pope. "I've got some good news and some bad news," God says. "I've decided that there should be one church and one religion. No more confusion."

The Pope says, "That's wonderful."

God says, "The bad news is, I'm calling from Salt Lake City."

"I'm lonely," Adam told God in the Garden of Eden. "I need to have someone around for company."

"Okay," replied God. "I'll give you the perfect companion. She is beautiful, intelligent, and gracious— she'll cook and clean for you and never say a cross word."

"Sounds great," Adam said. "But what's she going to cost?"

"An arm and a leg," answered God.

"That's pretty steep," replied Adam. "What can I get for a rib?"

A guy goes into confession and says to the priest, "Father, I'm eighty years old, married, have four kids and eleven grandchildren, and last night I had an affair and I made love to two eighteen-year-old girls. Both of them. Twice."

And the priest says, "Well, my son, when was the last time you were at confession?"

"Never, Father, I'm Jewish."

"So then, why are you telling me?"

"I'm tellin' everybody!"

This guy goes into his barber, and he's all excited. He says, "I'm going to go to Rome. I'm flying on Alitalia and staying at the Rome Hilton, and I'm going to see the Pope." The barber says, "Ha! Alitalia is a terrible airline, the Rome Hilton is a dump, and when you see the Pope, you'll probably be standing in back of about 10,000 people."

So the guy goes to Rome and comes back. His barber asks, "How was it?"

"Great," he says. "Alitalia was a wonderful airline. The hotel was great. And I got to meet the Pope."

"You met the Pope?" said the barber.

"I bent down to kiss the Pope's ring."

"And what did he say?"

"He said, 'Where did you get that crummy haircut?'"

Eve, in the Garden of Eden, said, "God, I have a problem. It's a beautiful garden, but I'm lonely and I'm sick of eating apples."

"Okay," God said. "I'll create a man for you."

Eve said, "What's a man?"

"He's a creature with aggressive tendencies and an enormous ego who doesn't listen and gets lost a lot, but he's big and strong, he can open jars and hunt animals, and he's fun in bed."

"Sounds great!" said Eve.

"There's just one other thing. He's going to want to believe I made him first."

What were the last words spoken at the Last Supper?

Everyone who wants to be in the picture, get on this side of the table.

Proof positive that Jesus was Irish:
1) He lived at home until he was 30.
2) The night before he died, he went out drinking with his buddies.
3) His mother thought he was God.
4) He thought his mother was a virgin.

Jesus was walking through the streets, and he noticed a group of people throwing stones at an adulteress. He stopped and said to the crowd, "Let the one who is without sin cast the first stone." All of a sudden, a big stone came out of the crowd and hit the woman right on the head. Jesus stopped, taken aback, then looked up and said, "Mom…!"

Every year, St. Peter conducted a tour down on earth. "This year," he told the Virgin Mary, "I'm going to survey all your shrines and compare them to the shrines I've seen in previous years." He took his tour and visited shrines around the world before he came back to heaven and reported to Mary, "I've got great news! There are more people at your shrines than anyone else's. But I noticed one thing—every single statue portrayed you with a sad expression on your face. Why is that?" And Mary said, "You might not understand my feelings." And St. Peter said, "Now, Mary, I've had many people tell me their innermost feelings—can't you open up to me?" And Mary said, "Well, you see, Peter…I really wanted a girl."

Why was Isaac twelve years old when God called Abraham to sacrifice his son?

Because if he had been a teenager, it wouldn't have been a sacrifice.

A guy enters the monastery. He has to take a vow of silence, but once a year he can write a word on the chalkboard in front of the head monk. The first year it's tough not to talk, but Word Day comes around and the monk writes "The" on the chalkboard. The second year is painful—it's very difficult not to talk—but finally Word Day rolls around. The monk scratches "food" on the chalkboard and enters his third year, which is excruciating. But the monk struggles through it, and when Word Day rolls around again, he writes "stinks." And the head monk says, "What's with you? You've been here for three years and all you've done is complain."

This man went to his rabbi and said, "I'm very troubled by my son. He went away and he came back a Christian."

The rabbi said, "You know, it's funny you say that. My son, too, left home and came back a Christian."

They decided to pray about it, and God said, "You know, it's funny you say that…"

Do you think that Moses led the Israelites through the desert for forty years because God was testing him, or because he wanted them to really appreciate the promised land when they finally got there, or because Moses refused to ask anybody for directions?

One morning the devil decided to go to church. He appeared suddenly, just before the offering, in a shower of flame and sparks and smoke. He ran up and down the aisle screaming, and all of the congregation ran out except for an old man sitting in back. The devil leaned over him, shook his spear, let out a ferocious roar, and cried, "I am Satan, Beelzebub, the Prince of Darkness. I am evil incarnate. Do you not fear me?"

The old man said, "Why should I? Been married to your sister for forty-eight years."

A man was praying to God. He said, "God!?"

God responded, "Yes?"

And the guy said, "Can I ask a question?"

"Go right ahead," God said.

"God, what is a million years to you?"

God said, "A million years to me is only a second."

"Hmm," the man wondered. Then he asked, "God, what is a million dollars worth to you?"

God said, "A million dollars to me is as a penny."

So the man said, "God, can I have a penny?"

And God said, "Sure!...Just a second."

Abraham decided to upgrade his PC to Windows '95 and Isaac couldn't believe it. He said, "Dad, your old PC doesn't have enough memory." And Abraham said, "My son, God will provide the RAM."

A nun comes into the office of the mother superior and whispers, "Mother superior, we…uh…we have discovered a case of syphilis."

"Wonderful. I was getting tired of the Chablis."

So Tommy goes into a confessional and says, "Bless me, Father, for I have sinned. I have been with a loose woman."

The priest says, "Is that you, Tommy?"

"Yes, Father, it is I."

"Who was the woman you were with?"

"I cannot tell you, Father, for I do not wish to ruin her reputation."

"Was it Brenda?"

"No, Father."

"Was it Fiona?"

"No, Father."

"Was it Ann?"

"No, Father."

"Very well, Tommy. Go say five Our Fathers and four Hail Marys."

Tommy goes back to his pew, and his buddy Sean slides over and asks, "What happened?"

And Tommy says, "I got five Our Fathers, four Hail Marys, and three good leads."

Do you know why you should always invite two Baptists to go fishing with you?

Because if you only invite one, he'll drink all your beer. Invite two and they won't drink any.

Two Baptist ministers are talking about the immorality of the country today, and one of them says, "I didn't sleep with my wife before I was married. How 'bout you?"

And the other says, "I don't know. What was her maiden name?"

The Lutheran minister is driving down to New York, and he's stopped in Connecticut for speeding. The state trooper smells alcohol on his breath and sees an empty wine bottle on the floor. He asks, "Sir, have you been drinking?"

And the minister says, "Just water."

The sheriff says, "Then why do I smell wine?"

The minister looks down at the bottle and says, "Good Lord, he's done it again!"

Three older Jewish mothers were sitting on a park bench in Miami Beach talking about how much their sons love them.

Sadie said, "You know the Manet painting hanging in my living room? My son, Irving, bought that for me for my seventy-fifth birthday. What a good boy he is, and how much he loves his mother."

Gertie said, "You call that love? You know that new Cadillac I just got for Mother's Day? That's from my son Bernie. What a doll."

Golda, in turn, replied, "That's nothing. You know my son Stanley? He's in analysis with a psychotherapist on Park Avenue. Five sessions a week—and what does he talk about? Me."

A maitre d' goes over to a middle-aged Jewish couple eating in his restaurant. He asks them, "Is anything all right?"

Why did the Amish couple get divorced?
  He was driving her buggy.

What goes CLOP CLOP CLOP, BANG BANG, CLOP CLOP CLOP?
  An Amish drive-by shooting.

Why don't Amish people water-ski?
  The horses would drown.

A pastor skips services one Sunday to go bear hunting in the mountains. As he turns the corner along the path, he and a bear collide. The pastor stumbles backwards, slips off the trail, and begins tumbling down the mountain with the bear in hot pursuit. Finally, the pastor crashes into a boulder, sending his rifle flying in one direction and breaking both of his legs. The pastor is lying there; he's lost his gun, and the bear is coming closer. So he cries out in desperation, "Lord, I repent for all I've done. Please make this bear a Christian." The bear skids to a halt at the pastor's feet, falls to its knees, clasps its paws together, and says, "Lord, I do thank you for the food I am about to receive."

Three couples—an elderly couple, a middle-aged couple, and a young newlywed couple—wanted to join a Baptist church. The pastor says, "We have special requirements for new parishioners. You must abstain from having sex for two weeks."

The couples agree and came back at the end of two weeks.

The pastor goes up to the elderly couple and asks, "Were you able to abstain from sex for the two weeks?"

The old man replies, "No problem at all, Pastor."

"Congratulations! Welcome to the church!" says the pastor.

The pastor goes to the middle-aged couple and asks, "Well, were you able to abstain from sex for the two weeks?"

The man replies, "The first week was not too bad. The second week I had to sleep on the couch for a couple of nights, but, yes, we made it."

"Congratulations! Welcome to the church," says the pastor.

The pastor then goes to the newlyweds and asks, "Well, were you able to abstain from sex for two weeks?"

"Well, Pastor, we were not able to go without sex for the two weeks," the young man replies.

"What happened?" inquires the pastor.

"My wife was reaching for a lightbulb on the top shelf and dropped it. When she bent over to pick it up, I couldn't help myself, and we had sex right there on the floor."

The pastor says, "Well, then, you're not welcome in the Baptist church."

"That's okay," says the young man. "We're not welcome at the grocery store anymore either."

LOSING MY RELIGION

The preacher was dissatisfied with how little his congregation put in the collection plates on Sundays, so he learned hypnosis. He began preaching his sermons in a monotone. He swung a watch slowly in front of the lectern, and at the end of the sermon he said, "Give!" and the collection plate was full of twenty-dollar bills. It worked for weeks. The congregation sat mesmerized during the sermon, staring at the watch swinging, and when he said, "Give!" they gave everything they had. Then one Sunday, at the end of the sermon, the chain on the watch broke, and the preacher said, "Oh, crap!"

This woman is visiting in Israel and notices that her little travel alarm needs a battery. She looks for a watch repair shop but she doesn't read Hebrew. Finally she sees a shop with clocks and watches in the window and goes in and hands the man her clock.

He says, "Madam, I don't repair clocks. I am a rabbi. I do circumcisions."

She says, "Why all the clocks in the window?"

And he says, "And what should I have in my window?"

A bum walked up to the Jewish mother on the street and said, "Lady, I haven't eaten in three days."

And the lady replied, "Try, honey. Force yourself."

This old guy was dying, and he said to his wife, "Honey, call for a priest." And she said, "But John, we're Lutheran."

And he said, "What? I should make Pastor Halvorson sick?"

A little boy and his grandmother were walking along the seashore when a huge wave appeared out of nowhere and swept the child out to sea. The grandmother, horrified, falls to her knees and says, "God, please return my beloved grandson. Please, I beg of you. Send him back safely." And, lo, another huge wave washed in and deposited the little boy on the sand at her feet. She picked him up, looked him over, and, looking up at the sky, said, "He had a hat!"

The drag queen walks into a Catholic church as the priest is coming down the aisle swinging the incense pot. And he says to the priest, "Oh, honey, I love your dress, but did you know your handbag's on fire?"

What's the difference between Jews and Christians?
    Jews get really angry, but Christians just get a little cross.

What is 666?
    That's the number of the beast.
    And 668?
    The next-door neighbor of the beast.
    What's 666-point-00000?
    That's the high-precision beast. And zero-point-666 is the Millibeast.
    And 1-900-666-6666 is where you can call and talk to a beast, live, one-on-one.
    And $665.95 is the retail price of the beast.
    $699.25 with 5 percent sales tax.
    $769.95 with all accessories.

Son: Mom, hi. How are you? How's everything in Florida?

Mom: Not too good. I've been very weak.

Son: Why are you weak?

Mom: Never mind.

Son: What's wrong?

Mom: Never mind. It's okay.

Son: Why are you weak, Mom?

Mom: I haven't eaten in thirty-eight days.

Son: That's terrible. Why haven't you eaten in thirty-eight days?

Mom: Because I didn't want my mouth to be filled with food if you should call.

Why was Jesus born in a manger?

Because Mary belonged to an HMO.

After church on Sunday morning, a young boy suddenly announced to his mother, "Mom, I've decided I'm going to be a minister when I grow up."

"That's okay with us," the mother said, "but what made you decide to be a minister?"

"Well," the boy replied, "I'll have to go to church on Sunday anyway, and I figure it will be more fun to stand up and yell."

A new pastor was out visiting his parishioners one Saturday afternoon. All went well until he came to one house. Although it was obvious someone was home, no one came to the door, even after he had knocked several times. Finally, he pulled out his card, wrote "Revelation 3:20" on the back, and stuck it in the door.

The next day as he was counting the offering he found his card in the collection plate. Below his message was the notation "Genesis 3:10."

Revelation 3:20 reads: "Behold I stand at the door, and knock: if any man hear my voice, and open the door, I will come in to him, and will dine with him, and he with me."

Genesis 3:10 reads: "And he said, I heard thy voice in the garden, and I was afraid, because I was naked."

A priest and a rabbi had been friends for many years. One evening over a cup of coffee the priest turned to the rabbi and said, "My friend, we've known each other for a long time, and there's something I've always wondered. Have you ever tasted ham?"

"Well," said the rabbi, looking a little sheepish, "I must admit, when I was a very young man and curious, I tasted some ham. Now tell me, my old friend," the rabbi said, "there's something I've always wondered. Have you ever been with a woman?"

"My friend," answered the priest, "I must confess, when I was a young man, before I entered the priesthood, yes, I was with a woman."

The rabbi smiled at the priest and said, "It's better than ham, isn't it?"

A man went to church, and afterward he stopped to shake the preacher's hand and say, "Preacher, I'll tell you, that was a damned fine sermon. Damned good."

The preacher said, "Thank you, sir, but I'd rather you didn't use that sort of language in the house of the Lord."

The man said, "I was so damn impressed with that sermon I put $5,000 in the collection plate."

The preacher said, "No shit?"

A man was so proud of his fancy new Cadillac that he invited a priest, a minister, and a rabbi to come and bless it. The priest approached the auto, sprinkled holy water over it, and chanted in Latin. The minister invoked the name of the almighty and led them all in silent prayer. The rabbi sang a psalm and cut off the end of the tailpipe.

Hyman Goldfarb went to Buckingham Palace to be knighted by the queen. When he knelt for her to put the sword on his shoulder, he was supposed to say something in Latin, but he forgot it.

So instead he said something in Hebrew, a question from the Passover seder, "Ma nishtana ha leila hazeh."

And the queen turned to her grand chamberlain and said, "Why is this knight different from all other knights?"

Our church is so liberal it's only open on Tuesdays.

Jews don't recognize Jesus, Protestants don't recognize the Pope, and Baptists don't recognize one another in the liquor store.

Two bees ran into each other. One asked the other how things were going.

The second bee said, "Really bad. Too much rain. No flowers or pollen."

The first bee said, "Here's what you do. Just fly down five blocks and turn left and keep going until you see all the cars. There's a bar mitzvah going on, and there are all kinds of fresh flowers and fresh fruit."

The second bee flew away, and a few hours later the two bees ran into each other again.

The first bee asked, "How'd it go?"

"Fine," said the second bee, "it was everything you said it would be."

"Uh, what's that thing on your head?" asked the first bee.

"That's my yarmulke," said the second bee. "I didn't want them to think I was a wasp."

A cruise ship sinks and three men make it to a desert island. The first man, a Catholic, kneels down and prays to the Lord to be saved from the island. The second man, a Lutheran, kneels down and prays to the Lord to be saved from the island. The third man, a Jew, says, "Hey. Two years ago I gave a million dollars to the Jewish Federation. Last year I gave two million. This year I pledged three million. Don't worry, they'll find me."

So the voter says to the politician, "I wouldn't vote for you if you were St. Peter himself."

"If I were St. Peter himself, you wouldn't be in my district."

The Christian fundamentalist family wanted to buy a Christian dog, so they found one that would fetch the Bible. And then when you told the dog to look up First Corinthians, it did it right away. And then when you didn't feel well, the dog would leap up on your lap and put a paw on your forehead and say, "Heel."

Why do Baptists object to fornication?
    They're afraid it might lead to dancing.

My son recently took up meditation. At least it's better than sitting doing nothing.

One of the angels asked God where he was going on vacation. He said, "Not Earth again. That's for sure. I went there about two thousand years ago, got a Jewish girl pregnant, and they haven't stopped talking about it since.

Adam and Eve had the perfect marriage. He didn't have to listen to her talk about men she knew before him, and she didn't have to put up with his mother.

Adam was the perfect figure of a man, and Eve was indescribably beautiful. So where do all the ugly people come from?

If there had been Three Wise Women who went to Bethlehem, they would have asked for directions, arrived on time, helped deliver the baby, cleaned the stable, made a meal, and brought some practical gifts.

A salesman from Budweiser went to the Vatican to get an audience with the pope, and he said, "Holy Father, I'm prepared to give you ten million dollars to change the words of the Lord's Prayer to 'give us this day our daily beer.'" The pope refused. "Okay, fifty million." The pope refused again, and the salesman said, "Okay, here's my card, call me if you change your mind." When the salesman left, the pope got on the phone and said, "Monsignor—it's me. Tell me, when does our contract with General Mills expire?"

The priest had his bicycle stolen and he thought somebody in his congregation might have done it, so the next Sunday he preached on the commandment "Thou shalt not steal," and then he noticed the commandment "Thou shalt not commit adultery," and then he remembered where he had left his bicycle.

The priest was caught fooling around with his housekeeper.

Apparently they found his vest in her pantry and her pants in his vestry.

As the prisoner was strapped to the electric chair, the priest said, "Son, is there anything I can do for you?"

The prisoner said, "Yeah, when they pull the switch, I'd like you to hold my hand."

Do you think it's okay to have sex before you're married, Father?

Not if it delays the ceremony.

A scientist wanted to find out once and for all if there was a God, so he built the most powerful computer ever and he accessed all imaginable data banks, all the libraries of the world, science institutes, universities, and scanned in every published book since the invention of the printing press. Finally, he sat down at his keyboard and typed in the question, "Is there a God?" And the computer said, "There is now."

The Jewish mother's telegram: "Begin worrying. Details follow."

Why do Jews always answer a question with another question?

Well, and why shouldn't we?

A Jewish man was seeing a psychiatrist for an eating and sleeping disorder. He said, "I am so obsessed with my mother... As soon as I go to sleep, I start dreaming, and everyone in my dream turns into my mother. I wake up in such a state, all I can do is go downstairs and eat a piece of toast."

The psychiatrist replies: "What, just one piece of toast, for a big boy like you?"

What do you get if you cross a Jehovah's Witness and a Unitarian?

Someone who goes around knocking on doors but isn't sure why.

A man goes to confession in Amsterdam:

Forgive me, Father, for I have sinned.

What is it, my son?

During World War II, I hid a Jew in my attic.

Well, that's not a sin. That's a good deed.

But I made him promise to pay me 20 guilders for every week he stayed.

Well, that's not good, but you did it for a good cause.

Okay, but I have one other question.

What is that, my son?

Do I have to tell him the war is over?

A man went to the doctor with two black eyes. The doctor said, "These are really bad. Were you in a fight or in an accident?"

The man replied, "I got these in church."

"In church!" the doctor replied. "How could that happen?"

"Well," the man explained, "we were kneeling at prayer. When we stood up, I noticed the woman in front of me had her skirt caught in between her butt cheeks. I thought it looked uncomfortable, so I reached over and tugged it out. She turned around and socked me."

"That explains one black eye," said the doctor. "How did you get the other one?"

"After she turned back around, I thought about it. I figured she didn't like what I had done, so I put it back."

BAR JOKES

A man walks into a bar with a chunk of asphalt under his arm and says, "Beer please, and one for the road."

So a five-dollar bill walks into a bar.
    The bartender says, "Get out-a here! We don't serve your type. This is a singles' bar."

A termite went into a bar and asked, "Is the bar tender here?"

A man walked into a bar looking sad, and the bartender asked him, "What's the matter?" The man said, "My wife and I had a fight, and she told me she wasn't going to speak to me for a month. And the month is up today."

This skeleton walks into a bar and says, "Give me a beer and give me a mop."

This fly walks into a bar, walks up to a woman sitting at the bar, and says, "I like that stool you're sitting on."

A Frenchman walks into a bar. He has a parrot on his shoulder, and the parrot is wearing a baseball cap. The bartender says, "Hey, that's neat—where did you get that?" And the parrot says, "France—they've got millions of them there."

"Hey, bartender. Pour me a cold one."

"Hey, go on, kid, you wanna get me in trouble?"

"Maybe later. Right now I just wanna beer."

An anteater walks into a bar and says that he'd like a drink.

"Okay," says the bartender. "How about a beer?"

"No-o-o-o-o-o-o-o-o-o," replies the anteater.

"Then how about a gin and tonic?"

"No-o-o-o-o-o-o-o-o-o."

"A martini?"

"No-o-o-o-o-o-o-o-o-o."

Finally, the bartender gets fed up and says, "Hey, buddy, if you don't mind me asking—why the long no's?"

A pair of jumper cables walked into a bar and asked for a drink.

The bartender said, "Okay, but I don't want you starting anything in here."

So there was this dyslexic guy who walked into a bra.

Charles Dickens walks into a bar and orders a martini.

The bartender asks, "Olive or Twist?"

A blind man walks into a bar, grabs his dog by its hind legs, and swings him around in a circle. The bartender says, "Hey buddy, what are you doing?"

And the blind man says, "Don't mind me, I'm just looking around."

Two ropes go into a bar. The bartender says, "Get out of here. We don't serve ropes in here."

The ropes go outside and one says to the other, "I have an idea." He ties himself up, messes up his hair, and goes back in. The bartender says, "Hey. No ropes." The rope says, "I'm not a rope."

The bartender says, "You're not a rope?"

"Nope. I'm a frayed knot."

Two guys were walking their dogs—one had a German shepherd and the other had a Chihuahua. The man with the shepherd suggested going into a bar for a drink. The other man says, "They're not going to let dogs into the bar." And the first guy says, "No? Watch this." He puts on some dark glasses, acts like the German shepherd is a Seeing Eye dog, walks into the bar, and orders a drink. And no one says anything.

So the second guy takes out some dark glasses, slips them on, and walks his Chihuahua into the bar. The bartender says, "Sorry—we don't allow dogs in here." And the man says, "It's okay—it's my Seeing Eye dog." The bartender laughs and says, "This Chihuahua is your Seeing Eye dog?" And the guy says, "They gave me a Chihuahua?"

Into the bar comes a grasshopper. And the bartender says, "Hey, we've got a drink named after you!"

And the grasshopper says, "Is that right? Why would anyone name a drink Bob?"

A horse walks into a bar. And the bartender says, "Why the long face?"

A cowboy walks into the bar and asks for a whiskey. Suddenly another cowboy rushes in and yells, "Joe, Joe, hurry up, your house is on fire!" The cowboy runs to the door and then stops and thinks, "Hey! I ain't got no house!"

The cowboy sits back down and drinks his whiskey. Suddenly another cowboy runs into the bar shouting, "Joe, Joe, hurry up, your father is dying!" The cowboy jumps up, runs out, jumps on his horse, and then remembers, "I ain't got no father!"

He walks back to the bar, sits down, and finishes his drink. And another cowboy bursts in and yells, "Joe, Joe, hurry up, you won the lottery and there's a million bucks for you at the post office!" The cowboy jumps to his feet, runs out of the bar, jumps on his horse, gallops to the post office, dashes in, and then he says, "Hey! My name ain't Joe!"

A guy comes in with a frog on his head, and the bartender says, "Where did you get that?" And the frog says, "It started out as a little bump on my butt."

This guy walks into a pub, sits down, and says, "Give me two beers. Rough day at work." And the bartender says, "Oh? What do you do?" The guy says, "I take care of the corgis—you know, the dogs the royal family owns."

The bartender says, "Tough job, huh?"

The guy says, "Well, all that inbreeding has led to low intelligence and bad temperament. And the dogs aren't that smart either."

A brain goes into a bar and says to the bartender, "I'll have a pint, please." The bartender says, "Sorry, I can't serve you, you're out of your head."

This guy walks into a bar and has a drink. And he looks in his pocket and orders another drink, looks in his pocket and orders another drink, looks in his pocket and orders another drink, looks in his pocket, and so on. And the bartender says, "What are you doing. What's in your pocket?" And the guy says, "It's a picture of my wife. When she starts looking good to me, I know it's time to go home."

A man goes into a bar and says, "Give me a drink before the trouble starts." And the bartender gives him a drink.

He drinks it and says, "Give me another drink before the trouble starts."

He downs that one and says, "Give me another drink before the trouble starts."

He drinks that and says, "Give me another drink before the trouble starts."

And the bartender says, "When's this trouble going to start?"

The man says, "The trouble starts as soon as you realize that I don't have any money."

The tourist goes into a bar, and there's a dog sitting in a chair, playing poker.

He says, "Is that dog really playing poker?" And the bartender says, "Yeah, but he's not too good. Whenever he has a good hand, he starts wagging his tail."

A pork chop goes into a bar and orders a drink.

The bartender says, "Sorry, you're food, and we don't serve food here."

This cowboy walks into a bar and orders a beer. His hat is made of brown wrapping paper, his shirt and vest are made of waxed paper, and his chaps, pants, and boots are made of paper. His spurs are made of tissue paper. Pretty soon they arrest him for rustling.

René Descartes is in a bar. At last call, the bartender asks him if he'd like another drink. Descartes says, "I think not." And he disappears.

A man walks into a bar. There's a beautiful woman sitting at the bar, and they sit and have a drink together. She leans over and says, "I want you to make me feel like a real woman." So he takes off his jacket and says, "I need this ironed."

A northerner walks into a bar down South around Christmastime, and there's a little nativity scene on the bar. And the guy says, "That's a nice nativity scene. But how come the three wise men are wearing firemen's hats?" And the bartender says, "Well, it says right there in the Bible—the three wise men came from a fire."

A pig walked into a bar, ordered fifteen beers, and drank them. The bartender asked, "Would you like to know where the bathroom is?"

"No," said the little pig. "I'm the little pig that goes wee-wee-wee all the way home."

A bear walks into a bar and says, "I'd like a beer and.........a packet of peanuts." The barman says, "Why the big pause?"

A panda walks into a bar, sits down, and orders a sandwich. He eats the sandwich, pulls out a gun, and shoots the waiter dead. As the panda stands up to go, the bartender shouts, "Hey! Where are you going? You just shot my waiter, and you didn't pay for your sandwich." The panda yells back at the bartender, "Hey man, I'm a *panda*. Look it up!"

The bartender opens his dictionary to "panda" and reads: "A tree-dwelling marsupial of Asian origin, characterized by distinct black and white coloring. Eats shoots and leaves."

This duck walks into a bar, and the bartender looks at him and says, "Hey, buddy, your pants are down around your ankles!"

A drunk guy walks into a bar and looks up to see a lady with a French poodle. The drunk slurs, "Where did you get that pig?"

The lady, with a look of surprise, snaps back, "I'll have you know that it is a Frrrench poodle."

The drunk looks at her and says, "I was talking to the French poodle."

A guy goes into a bar, orders four shots of the most expensive thirty-year-old single-malt Scotch, and downs them one after the other.

The barkeep says, "You look like you're in a hurry."

"You would be too if you had what I have," says the guy.

"What have you got?" asks the bartender.

"Fifty cents."

This duck waddles into a bar, and the bartender says, "What can I get for you?" The duck says, "Got any grapes?" The bartender says, "No, we serve beer and whiskey and stuff like that." The duck says, "Okay," and he leaves.

The next day, the same duck comes in, hops up on the stool, and says, "Got any grapes?" The bartender say, "No—I've told you two days in a row that we don't have any grapes. You come in here again and I'm going to nail your beak to the bar!" So the duck leaves.

The very next day, the same duck comes back into the bar and says, "Got any nails?" The bartender says, "No, why?" And the duck says, "Got any grapes?"

A man walks out of a bar and sees a bum panhandling on the corner. And the bum says, "Mister, do you have a dollar you could spare me?"

The man thinks about the question for a bit and asks the bum, "If I give you a dollar, are you going to use it to buy liquor?"

"No," says the bum.

The man then asks the bum, "If I give you a dollar, are you going to use it for gambling?"

Again the bum says, "No."

So the man says to the bum, "Do you mind coming home with me so I can show my wife what happens to someone who doesn't drink or gamble?"

Waiter: And how did you find your steak, sir?
Diner: Well, I just pushed aside a pea and there it was...

A salesman walks into the bar and asks, "You know where Bubba lives?"

"Sure," says the bartender, and he gives him directions. "But you gotta be careful. Don't honk your horn when you pull up in front of Bubba's house."

"Why not?" asks the salesman.

"Well, you see, about three months ago, Bubba's wife ran off with a banjo player named Junior. And every time Bubba hears somebody honk, he's afraid the banjo player is bringing her back."

A drunk staggers out of a bar and into a nearby cathedral. He eventually stumbles his way down the aisle and into a confessional. After a lengthy silence, the priest asks, "May I help you, my son?" "I dunno," comes the drunk's voice from behind the partition. "You got any toilet paper on your side?"

A thief breaks into a bar and is heading right for the cash register when he hears a voice behind him say, "God is watching." He turns around, but he doesn't see anything, so he goes back to the cash register. Again he hears, "God is watching." So he turns around and sees a parrot over in the corner. He goes over to it and says, "What's your name?"

"John the Baptist," replies the bird.

"That's a funny name for a parrot," says the thief. "Who named you that?"

The parrot says, "My owner. The same guy who named the Rottweiler God."

This old couple walk into the bar, and the husband goes over and starts flirting with some young women. And the bartender says to the wife, "Doesn't it bother you that your husband is always making passes at the younger women around here?"

"No, no, no, not really," the wife says. "I mean, dogs chase cars, but that doesn't mean they know how to drive."

This guy goes into a bar and orders three separate shot glasses of Irish whiskey.

He drinks all three. He does this day after day after day, and the bartender finally says, "You know, I can put all three of those shots into one glass for you."

The guy says, "No, I prefer it this way. See, I have two brothers—they're over in Ireland, and I love them. This glass right here is for Finnian and this one here is for Fergus, and this one is for me. This way I can feel like we're all here together having a drink."

And the guy continues to come in day after day after day, and the bartender continues to set up three glasses. Then one day, the guy says, "Give me two shots today."

"What happened? Did something happen to one of your brothers?" the bartender asks.

"No, no, no," the guy says. "They're okay. It's just that I decided to quit drinking."

A man walked into a bar carrying an ape in his arms. "I just bought this fella as a pet," he explained. "We have no children, so he's going to live with us, just like one of the family. He'll eat at our table, even sleep in the bed with me and the wife." "But what about the smell?" someone asked. "Oh, he'll just have to get used to it, the same way I did."

A man walked into a bar, sat down, and ordered a beer. As he sipped the beer he heard a soothing voice say, "Nice tie." Looking around he noticed that the bar was empty except for himself and the bartender at the end of the bar. A few sips later the voice said, "Beautiful shirt." At this, the man called the bartender over. "Hey, I must be losing my mind," he told him. "I keep hearing these voices saying nice things, and there's not a soul in here but us."

"It's the peanuts," answered the bartender.

"Say what?"

"You heard me. It's the peanuts…they're complimentary."

Three mice walked into a bar. The first mouse had a shot of whiskey and said, "When I see a mousetrap, I lie on my back and set it off with my foot. When the bar comes down, I catch it in my teeth, bench-press it twenty times to work up an appetite, and then make off with the cheese."

The second mouse drank two shots of whiskey and said, "Yeah, well, when I see rat poison, I collect as much as I can, take it home, grind it up into a powder, and add it to my coffee each morning so I can get a good buzz going for the rest of the day."

The third mouse said, "I can't stay long. I've got a date with the cat."

124

A man walks into a bar and orders a beer. He sips it and sets it down. A monkey swings across the bar and pisses in the pint. The man asks the barman who owns the monkey. The barman indicates the piano player. The man walks over to the piano player and says, "Do you know your monkey pissed in my beer?" The pianist replies, "No, but if you hum it I'll play it."

A cowboy walks out of a bar and a second later comes back in, mighty mad. "Okay," he growls. "Now which one of you sidewindin' hombres went outside an' painted mah horse bright red while I was a-drinkin'?"

Nobody answers, and the cowpoke draws his six-shooter and yells, "*I said which one of you mangy polecats painted mah horse red?!*"

Slowly one of the cowboys at the bar stands up. He is six feet, nine inches tall, and he pulls a small cannon from his holster. "I done it," he growls.

The first cowboy puts his gun back in the holster and says, "Just wanted to let you know the first coat's dry."

A man walks into the bar with a giraffe. He says, "A beer for me, and one for my giraffe." And they stand around drinking for hours, until the giraffe passes out on the floor. The man pays his tab and gets up to leave, and the bartender says, "Hey! You're not going to leave that lyin' on the floor, are you?"

The man says, "That's not a lion, it's a giraffe."

DRINK & BE MERRY

A Texan walks into a pub in Ireland and clears his voice to the crowd of drinkers. He says, "I hear you Irish are a bunch of drinkers. I'll give 500 American dollars to anybody in here who can drink ten pints of Guinness back-to-back." The room is quiet, and no one takes the Texan's offer. One man even leaves. Thirty minutes later the same gentleman who left shows up and taps the Texan on the shoulder. "Is your bet still good?" asks the Irishman. The Texan says yes and asks the bartender to line up ten pints of Guinness. Immediately the Irishman tears into all ten of the pint glasses, drinking them all back-to back. The other pub patrons cheer as the Texan sits in amazement. The Texan gives the Irishman the $500 and says, "If ya don't mind me askin', where did you go for that thirty minutes you were gone?" The Irishman replies, "Oh…I went to the pub down the street to see if I could do it first."

A redneck swaggers into a bar. "Hey barkeep, set me up with a cold one," he says. Then he looks to the end of the bar and asks the bartender, "Hey, is that Jesus down there?" The barkeep nods. "Well, set him up with a cold one, too."

As Jesus gets up to leave, he walks over to the redneck, touches him, and says, "For your kindness, you are healed!"

The redneck jumps back and exclaims, "Don't touch me! I'm drawing disability!"

Four brewery presidents walk into a bar. The guy from Corona sits down and says, "Hey, Señor, I would like the world's best beer, a Corona." The bartender gives it to him.

The guy from Budweiser says, "I'd like the best beer in the world. Give me 'The King of Beers,' a Budweiser." The bartender gives him one.

The guy from Coors says, "I'd like the only beer made with Rocky Mountain spring water. Give me a Coors." He gets it.

The guy from Guinness sits down and says, "Give me a Coke." The bartender is a little taken aback, but gives him what he ordered.

The other brewery presidents look over at him and ask, "Why aren't you drinking a Guinness?"

The Guinness president replies, "Well, I figured if you guys aren't drinking beer, neither would I."

A man walked into a bar and sat down next to a man with a dog at his feet. "Does your dog bite?" he asked. "No," was the reply. So he reaches down to pet the dog, and the dog bites him. "I thought you said your dog doesn't bite!" he said. "That's not my dog!"

A dog walks into a bar and says, "Hey, guess what? I'm a talking dog. Ever seen a talking dog before? How about a drink for the talking dog?"

The bartender answers, "OK. The toilet's right around the corner."

A mangy looking guy goes into a bar and orders a drink. The bartender says, "No way. I don't think you can pay for it." The guy says, "You're right. I don't have any money, but if I show you something you haven't seen before, will you give me a drink?" The bartender says, "Only if what you show me ain't risqué." "Deal!" says the guy, and reaches into his coat pocket and pulls out a hamster. He puts the hamster on the bar, and it runs to the end of the bar, down off the bar, across the room, up the piano, jumps on the keyboard, and starts playing Gershwin songs. And the hamster is really good. The bartender says, "You're right. I've never seen anything like that before. That hamster is truly good on the piano."

The guy downs the drink and asks the bartender for another. "Money or another miracle, else no drink," says the bartender.

The guy reaches into his coat again and pulls out a frog. He puts the frog on the bar, and the frog starts to sing. He has a marvelous voice and great pitch. A fine singer. A stranger from the other end of the bar runs over to the guy and offers him $300 for the frog. The guy says, "It's a deal." He takes the $300 and gives the stranger the frog. The stranger runs out of the bar.

The bartender says to the guy, "Are you some kind of nut? You sold a singing frog for $300? It must have been worth millions." "Not so," says the guy. "The hamster is also a ventriloquist."

A well-dressed young businessman walks into a bar. The bartender asks, "What can I get you?" The well-dressed man replies, "I'll have a glass of twelve-year-old Scotch." The bartender returns with the drink. The man takes a sip, winces, and spits it out, exclaiming, "That's ten-year-old Scotch! How dare you insult a man of my stature with inferior Scotch!" The bartender explains that the bar doesn't carry twelve-year-old Scotch, and he had thought the man wouldn't notice the two-year difference.

The well-dressed man next asks for fifteen-year-old bourbon. The bartender returns with the drink. The man takes a sip, winces, and spits it out, exclaiming, "That's twelve-year-old bourbon! How dare you insult a man of my stature with inferior bourbon." The bartender apologizes, citing his earlier explanation. The situation repeats itself regarding the well-dressed man's next request, this time for a glass of thirty-year-old port wine.

Meanwhile, an old drunk at the end of the bar calls the bartender down and produces a glass. Handing the glass to the bartender, he says, "Give this to that well-dressed man, and tell him it's on me."

The bartender gives the drink to the well-dressed man, indicating the old drunk at the end of the bar. The man takes a sip, winces, and spits it out. "My Lord!" he cries. "That tastes like urine!"

"It is," replies the old drunk. "Now tell me how old I am."

A woman walked into a bar and asked for a double entendre. So the barman gave her one.

A man walks into a bar with a newt on his shoulder. He told the bartender that the newt's name was Tiny.

"Why?" asks the bartender.

"Because he's my newt!"

This baby seal walks into a bar and the bartender says "What'll ya have..."

The seal says, "Anything but a Canadian Club..."

A pickle walks into a bar and the bartender says, "Hey, you're a pickle! What are you doing here?"

The pickle says, "Well, for starters, I'm celebrating the fact that I can walk."

A priest, a rabbi, a lawyer, a redneck, a blonde, and a dog walk into a bar. The bartender looks up and says, "Is this some kind of joke?"

A man walks into a bar and asks the bartender, "Do you have any Campari?"

The bartender says, "Do I have Campari! Look down here!" And he takes him to the basement and there's a hundred cases of Campari.

"Boy, you must sell a lot of Campari."

"No, but the man who sells me Campari—he sells a lot of Campari."

A man walks into a bar and says, "I know the sign says No Smoking but would you mind if I smoke in here?"

"It's okay with me. Just make sure you put the lit end into your mouth."

A man walked out of the bar and got in his car and a policeman came over.

"Sir, your eyes seem to be bloodshot. Have you been drinking?"

"Officer, your eyes seem to be glazed. Have you been eating doughnuts?"

A cowboy is sitting at a bar. A guy came and sat next to him and looked at the cowboy hat and asked, "Are you a real cowboy?"

The cowboy replied, "Yes, I believe I am a real cowboy. I spend my day riding around on a horse, looking after cattle and sleeping under the stars."

Later, a girl came and sat next to him and asked, "Are you a real cowboy?"

"Yes, I spend my entire day riding around on the range looking after horses and cattle, I suppose I am a cowboy. What about you? What are you?"

"I'm a lesbian. I spend my whole day thinking about women. I get up in the morning, I have a shower and I think about women, I have breakfast and I think about women, I go to work and I think about women."

Ten minutes later, another guy comes and sits next to the cowboy and asks, "Are you a real cowboy?"

"Well, ten minutes ago, I thought I was."

An Irishman walked into a bar, and there was a little brass lamp at the end of the bar. He touched it, and a genie came out and gave him three wishes. He said, "Ah, faith! I wish for a bottle of Guinness that will never run dry." Poof! A bottle appears, and he drinks it, and holds it up and it magically fills itself up again. He drinks it down, it refills again, then the genie asks, "And what are your other two wishes?"

"Just give me two more like this one."

A penguin walked into a bar and said, "Has my father been in here today?"

The bartender said, "I don't know. What does he look like?"

A man walked into the bar and ordered a drink, and the bartender said, "I thought you quit drinking."

"No, I just wanted to cut my drinking in half, so I joined A."

ADULTS-ONLY JOKES

Sex is *not* the answer. Sex is the question. The answer is *yes*!

It's only premarital sex if you're intending to get married.

Do you go for casual sex, or should I dress up?

Why don't women blink during foreplay?
     They don't want to miss it.

The Lord created alcohol so that ugly people would have a chance to have sex.

Sex on television can't hurt you unless you fall off.

According to Sigmund Freud, what comes between fear and sex?
     Fünf.

Did you hear about the thieves who stole an entire shipment of Viagra?
     Police are looking for a gang of hardened criminals.

An old lady who never married specified in her will that her tombstone say, "Born a virgin, lived a virgin, died a virgin." That was too many words to put on the stone so they just wrote, "Returned unopened."

A psychologist did a study of 300 people and their sex lives. Some of them said they had sex almost every night, others said they had sex once a week, and others said they had sex once or twice a month. One man said he had sex only once a year. The psychologist felt bad for him and went over, patted him on the back, and said, "That's too bad. I'm really sorry for you." The man grinned up at him and said, "Yes, but tonight's the night."

"Hi. Couldn't help but notice the book you're reading."

"Yes, it's about finding sexual satisfaction. It's interesting. Did you know that, statistically, American Indian and Polish men are the best lovers? By the way, my name is Jill. What's yours?"

"Flying Cloud Kowalski. Nice to meet you."

Three women were returning to their Hungarian village when they spotted a man, obviously very inebriated, walking ahead of them. As they watched, he stumbled and fell face down into a mud puddle. When they walked up to him, one woman turned him over to see if she recognized him. However, his face was so covered with mud she couldn't tell, so she bent over and unzipped his pants. She remarked, "Well, he's not my husband." The second woman, peering over the first woman's shoulder, agreed, "You're right, he's not your husband." The third woman, somewhat older than the other two, bent over to look and said, "He's not even from our village."

A dedicated shop steward is at a convention in Las Vegas and decides to go into a brothel. He asks the madam, "Is this a union house?"

"No, it's not," she replies.

"So, how much do the girls earn?" the union man asks.

"Well, if you pay me $100, the house gets $80 and I pay the girl $20."

The man says, "That's terrible!" He stomps out. Finally he finds a brothel where the madam says, "Yes, this is a union house."

"And if I pay you $100, what cut does the girl get?"

"She gets $80."

"That's great!" the man says. "I'd like Tiffany."

"I'm sure you would," says the madam, "but Ethel here has seniority."

Three women go out to a nightclub to see male dancers. One of the women wants to impress the others, so she pulls out a $10 bill and waves the dancer over. She licks the $10 bill and sticks it to his left buttock. Not to be outdone, the second woman pulls out a $20 bill, licks it, and slaps it on the other cheek. The dancer looks down at the third woman and raises his eyebrows. Thinking for a minute, she reaches into her purse. She pulls out her ATM card, swipes it down the crack, grabs the $30, and goes home.

Did you hear about the guy who had sex with his canary?

Came down with a bad case of chirpies. And the worst thing about it is it's untweetable.

A teenage couple had been dating for a couple of weeks, and the relationship seemed to be going rather well. The young girl told the boy that if he were to come over for dinner, meet the parents, and make a good impression, she would reward him by making love to him.

Well, he was pretty excited, as it would be their first time, and he immediately went down to the local pharmacy to buy some condoms. But, it being his first time, he didn't know what kind to buy, so he asked the pharmacist for help. The pharmacist spent a good hour discussing the different kinds of condoms, what they do, how to pick a size, etc. He then asked the boy which he would like. To which the boy responded, "Well, being as it is going to be the first time, why don't I get the family pack." The pharmacist rang it up and sent him on his way.

Finally the night arrived. Of course the boy was very nervous but was determined to make a good lasting impression on the girl's parents. Everyone sat down to dinner, and the mother said, "Let us bow our heads and pray." Everyone bowed their heads and said grace. When they were finished, everyone looked up…except the boy. He continued to bow his head and mumble in prayer. After about twenty minutes, he is still praying and the girl taps him on the leg and whispers, "I never knew you were so religious." And the boy says, "I never knew your dad was a pharmacist!"

What is the similarity between Viagra and Disney World?
You have to wait an hour for a three-minute ride.

A man goes into a restaurant. A beautiful waitress comes over to serve him and asks what he would like. He says, "I want a quickie."

She slaps him and says, "Just give me your order, mister!"

The man says, "I want a quickie!"

She slaps him again. "Last chance," she says. "What do you want?"

The man insists, "Look, I really, really want a quickie!"

Another customer leans over and says, "I believe that's pronounced *quiche*."

An old woman is sitting in a rocking chair on her porch, petting her cat, Puff. A fairy appears and says, "I'm here to give you three wishes."

The old woman says, "I wish I were twenty-one years old and beautiful again." Poof! She is.

"Now I wish I had a million dollars and this old house were a mansion." Poof! Done.

"And now, I wish that Puff were the handsomest man in the world and deeply in love with me."

Poof! Suddenly she's in the arms of the handsomest man in the world. He kisses her and says, "Darling, aren't you sorry you had me fixed?"

A traveling salesman stops at the the nearest farmhouse and asks if he can spend the night. The farmer says okay and tells him he can go upstairs and sleep in the same room as his daughter. The salesman goes upstairs and, as he enters the daughter's room, notices another salesman in bed with her. "Oh, my God!" he proclaims. "I must be in the wrong joke!"

Mama Stork, Papa Stork, and Baby Stork sat down to dinner and Mama said, "What did you do today, Papa?"

And Papa said, "I was out making someone very happy."

And Mama said, "I was out making someone very happy, too. What were you doing, Baby?"

And Baby Stork said, "I was out scaring the crap out of college students."

A lady who lived in a small Minnesota town had two pet monkeys she was very fond of. One of them took sick and died. A couple of days later the other one died of a broken heart. Wishing to keep them, the kindly lady took them to the taxidermist. The man asked her if she would like them mounted. "Oh, no," she replied, "just have them holding hands."

Three engineers are arguing about which is better, mechanical, electrical, or civil engineering. The mechanical engineer says, "God must've been a mechanical engineer: look at the joints in the human body." The second says, "No, God must've been an electrical engineer: look at the nervous system." And the third says, "God had to be a civil engineer: who else would've run a waste disposal pipeline right through a great recreational area?"

Mrs. Johnson had quintuplets. Isn't that something? Did you know that happens only once in four million times?

My gosh, when did they ever have time to go to work?

What do you get when you take Viagra with beans?
   A stiff wind.

There were a lot of Viagra jokes a few years ago, but they
seem to have petered out.

A woman approaches a man in a bar and says, "Hi. You
look lonely. I'll do anything you want for two hundred
dollars." The guy says, "Okay, how about you paint my
house?"

I had an uncle who was so dumb, the closest he ever got to
a 4.0 was his blood alcohol content.

My uncle peed in a wheat field once and was arrested for
going against the grain.

Excuse me, would you mind giving up your seat? I'm
pregnant.
   Certainly. But I must say, you don't look pregnant.
   Well, it's only been about half an hour.

On the chest of a barmaid at Yale
Were tattooed the prices of ale
And on her behind
For the sake of the blind
Was the same information in Braille

Daddy, Megan and I want to get married.

I see, Danny. Well, how will you support her?

I get two dollars allowance each week, and she gets an allowance too.

But what if there's a baby?

So far, we've been lucky.

Son, I think it's time we talked about sex.

Sure, Dad. What do you want to know?"

TOTALLY TASTELESS JOKES

What's green and red and goes fifty miles per hour?
A frog in a blender.

Why do farts smell?
So that deaf people can enjoy them, too!

So these two cannibals are eating a clown and one says, "Does this taste funny to you?"

Did you hear about the cannibal who passed his brother in the woods one day?

Two cannibals were sitting by a fire and one says, "Gee, I hate my mother-in-law."
And the other says, "So, try the potatoes."

Why did the cannibal eat the tightrope walker?
He wanted a balanced meal.

Two guys are captured by cannibals. They're stuck naked in a big pot of water over a fire, and the water gets hotter and hotter. All of a sudden, one guy starts laughing, and the other guy says, "What's so funny?"
"I just peed in their soup!"

Did you hear about the cannibal who was expelled from school?
He was buttering up his teacher.

Two cannibals meet one day. The first cannibal says, "You know, I just can't seem to get a tender missionary. I've baked them, I've roasted them, I've stewed them, I've barbecued them, I've tried every sort of marinade. I just can't seem to get them tender."

The second cannibal asks, "What kind of missionary do you use?"

The other replies, "You know, the ones that hang out at that place at the bend of the river. They have those brown cloaks with a rope around the waist, and they're sort of bald on top with a funny ring of hair on their heads."

"Aha!" the second cannibal replies. "No wonder—those are friars!"

Have you noticed how bad Stan's breath is?

Are you kidding? It's so bad, people look forward to his farts!

They announced today that the Green Bay Packers and the Tampa Bay Buccaneers are going to merge and form one team called the Tampacks. It may be a mediocre team, though. It'll only be good for one period and there'll be no second string.

What do you get when you mix holy water with castor oil?

A religious movement!

What happened to the fly on the toilet seat?

He got pissed off!

A guy walked into a cafe and asked for a bowl of chili. The waitress said, "The guy next to you got the last bowl." He looks over and sees that the guy's bowl of chili is full. He says, "If you're not going to eat that, mind if I take it?" The other guy says, "No, help yourself." He starts to eat it and about halfway down, his fork hits something. It's a dead mouse, and he vomits the chili back into the bowl. The other guy says, "That's about as far as I got, too."

A woman goes to the store to buy some fishing gear for the weekend. She asks an employee for any suggestions. A blind man who works at the store suggests a rod and reel costing $20. She agrees and moves to the counter to pay for her purchase.

The blind man walks behind the counter to the register. In the meantime the woman breaks wind. At first she is embarrassed, but then she realizes there is no way he could tell it was her. Being blind, he wouldn't know she was the only person around. He rings up the sale and says, "That will be $25.50."

She says, "But didn't you say it was $20?"

He says, "Yes ma'am. The rod and reel is $20, the duck call is $3, and the catfish stink bait is $2.50."

Why does Piglet smell so bad?
He always plays with Pooh.

Did you know diarrhea is hereditary? It runs in your genes.

What's invisible and smells like carrots?
Rabbit farts.

The Queen was showing the Archbishop of Canterbury around the royal stables when one of the stallions farted so loudly it couldn't be ignored. "Oh dear," said the Queen. "How embarrassing. I'm frightfully sorry about that."

"It's quite understandable," said the Archbishop, adding after a moment, "As a matter of fact, I thought it was the horse."

What's the difference between boogers and broccoli?

Kids won't eat broccoli.

Two airline mechanics get off work at LaGuardia, and one says, "Let's go have a beer." The other says, "Why don't we try drinking jet fuel? I hear it tastes like whiskey, and you don't have any hangover in the morning." So they drink about a quart of it apiece. It tastes great and they have a good time. The next morning, one of them calls up the other and says, "Hey, how do you feel?"

"I feel great."

"Me, too. No hangover."

"Just one thing. Have you farted yet?"

"No…"

"Well, don't. I'm calling from Phoenix!"

A man walks into his house with a handful of dog turds, and he says to his wife, "Look what I almost stepped in!"

Did you hear about the blind skunk who fell in love with a fart?

There was this woman who had a problem with silent gas. She went to the doctor and she said, "This is so embarrassing. I have this problem of farting silently. You probably haven't noticed, but I've let three of them since I've been in this office with you. Is there anything you can do?"

He said, "Yes, but the first thing is to get you fitted for a hearing aid."

What is the difference between a saloon and an elephant's fart?

One is a barroom and the other is a BARRRROOOOOOOM!

There once was a blind man who decided to visit Texas. When he got on the plane, he felt the seats and said, "Wow, these seats are big!" The person next to him answered, "Everything is big in Texas." When he finally arrived in Texas, he decided to visit a restaurant. Upon arriving he ordered a drink and got a mug placed between his hands. He exclaimed, "Wow, these mugs are big!" The bartender replied, "Everything is big in Texas."

After a couple of drinks, the blind man asked the bartender where the bathroom was located. The bartender replied, "Second door to the right." The blind man headed for the bathroom but accidentally tripped and passed by the second door. Instead, he entered the third door, which led to the swimming pool, and he fell into the pool. Scared to death, the blind man started shouting, "Don't flush, don't flush!"

"Gladys, it's like a miracle. Every night when I get up and go to the bathroom, God turns the light on for me, and when I'm finished, he turns the light off."

"Harry—you're doing it in the refrigerator again!"

So, Professor, you're back from the Rawalpindi archipelago, huh? Discover anything interesting out there?

Yes. The tribe has discovered a kind of palm frond that can be made into suppositories to cure constipation.

Do they really work?

Hey, with fronds like those, who needs enemas?

What did the elephant say to the naked man?

"It's cute, but can you really breathe through that thing?"

How did Helen Keller burn her ear?

She answered the iron.

How did she burn her other ear?

They called back.

How did Helen Keller burn her fingers?

She tried to read the waffle iron.

Why are Helen Keller's stockings yellow?

Because her seeing-eye dog can't see either.

Why can't Helen Keller drive?

Because she's a woman.

146

Why do you feel so sophisticated when you're in the bathroom?

European.

This sailor met a pirate in a bar, and the sailor couldn't help but notice that the pirate was pretty badly the worse for wear. He had a peg leg, and a hook, and an eyepatch.

So the sailor asked the pirate how he got the peg leg, and the pirate answered, "Well, matey, I got washed overboard one night while we was in a fierce storm. An' dern me if a shark didn't go and bite off me leg."

Then the sailor asked, "So how'd you get the hook?"

And the pirate answered, "Well, we was in a fierce fight while boarding a ship one time, and that's when I got me hand cut off."

Finally, the sailor asked, "So how'd you get the eyepatch?"

And the pirate responded, "A seagull pooped in me eye."

And the sailor said, "You mean to tell me you lost an eye just because a seagull pooped in it?"

The pirate said, "Well, it was the first day I had me hook."

My company put me up in a pretty low-class hotel. I called the front desk and said, "I've got a leak in my sink."

They said, "Go ahead."

Did you hear about the Easter egg hunt for the Alzheimer's patients?

They hid their own eggs.

What drove the thirty-nine members of Heaven's Gate to suicide?

You put that many people together, force them to work in Windows '95, and it's bound to happen.

(I heard some of them were UNIX programmers.)

This lieutenant is leading his troops into battle, and his sergeant says, "Sir, there's a whole platoon of enemy coming toward us." And the lieutenant says, "All right, sergeant, bring my red shirt." So the lieutenant puts on his red shirt, and the troops go into battle. They move forward against the enemy.

The next day, the sergeant says, "Sir, there's a whole regiment of enemy coming toward us." And the lieutenant says, "All right, sergeant, bring my red shirt." So the sergeant brings him his shirt, and they move forward and defeat the enemy. And that night, a young private asks, "Lieutenant, why do you always wear this red shirt in battle?" The lieutenant says, "Because, son, if I should be wounded, I don't want my men to see the blood and be demoralized." And the private says, "Oh, gosh," and thinks the lieutenant is a really courageous guy.

The next day, the sergeant comes running to the lieutenant all agitated. He says, "Sir, there are two regiments of the enemy moving toward us, and they have tanks and heavy artillery and…"

The lieutenant interrupts, "Sergeant, bring me my brown pants!"

Four big executives are playing golf together. On the second tee they hear a phone ring, and Michael Eisner reaches into his golf bag, pulls out a cellular phone, and talks to his office awhile.

They play the second hole. On the third tee there's a little buzz. Warren Buffet puts one finger in his ear and one finger to his mouth and talks. Afterward he explains that he has a tiny microphone installed in one fingernail and a tiny speaker in another, so he can keep in touch with the office. Everyone is impressed.

They play the third hole. On the fourth tee, Ted Turner starts talking—no phone or anything. Afterward he explains that he has a microphone in a filling in his tooth and a speaker in his ear, so he can always talk to the office. They are even more impressed and move on.

Suddenly they see Bill Gates pull his pants down, squat, and reach into his golf bag for a roll of toilet paper. He looks up and says, "It's okay. I'm expecting a fax."

Why do airlines say that in case of an emergency water landing, the seat cushions can be used as a floatation device? If we're going down, my seat cushion's going to be used as a toilet.

Did you know that in 1553, the Norwegians invented the toilet seat?

Really?

Yeah. Later, the Italians invented the hole in the middle of it.

149

A county extension agent is visiting a farm and needs to use the toilet, but he remembers that there is no running water. So he runs around back to the outhouse, opens the door, and the hired man is sitting there. But the hired man says, "It's okay. Come on in, it's a two-holer." So the agent goes in and sits down. Soon, the hired man stands up, and as he pulls up his pants, some change tumbles out of his pocket and goes down the hole. The hired man shakes his head, pulls out his wallet, and drops a ten-dollar bill down the hole. The extension agent says, "What did you do that for?" And the hired man says, "Well, I ain't goin' down there for just thirty-five cents."

I was at this banquet and my false teeth were hurting me, so the guy sitting next to me reaches into his pocket and pulls out some dentures, and says, "Try these." So I do. But they're too tight. He gives me another set, he says, "Try these." I try them and they're fine. I wear them for the rest of the banquet, then I give them back. I say, "Thanks. Lucky for me I was sitting next to a dentist." He says, "No, I'm an undertaker."

I went out with twins last night.
   Really? Did you have a good time?
   Well—Yes and no.

As the drunk said as he leaned over the toilet, "Two beers, coming up!"

Do you prefer port or sherry, sir?

Port, by all means. To me, port is the apotheosis of wine. A glass of vintage port is almost orchestral in its complexity, and between the bouquet and the finish, there is such a panoply of colors, of tonal textures. And sherry makes me fart.

What do you call a woman with no arms or legs on a bar-b-que grill?

Patty.

A man with no arms or legs on a bar-b-que grill?

Frank.

One who lives in a bush?

Russell.

A man with no arms and no legs hanging on the wall?

Art.

One in a swimming pool?

Bob.

...in a ditch?

Phil.

What do you call a guy with no feet?

Neil.

What do you call a woman with one leg shorter than the other?

Eileen.

What if she's Asian?

Irene.

What do you call a man with a seagull on his head?
   Cliff.

What do you call a man with a spade in his head?
   Doug.

What's different about a bulimic's birthday party?
   The cake jumps out of the girl.

The man went to his proctologist and there on the examining table was a tube of K-Y jelly, a pair of rubber gloves, and a bottle of beer. What's the beer for?
   It's a butt light.

How can you tell if a woman is wearing panty hose?
   If she farts, her ankles swell.

What did the maxi-pad say to the fart?
   You are the wind beneath my wings.

How do you make a dog drink?
   Put it in a blender.

How do you make a dog go meow?
   Freeze it and then run it through a band saw.

What goes "Marc! Marc!"?
   A dog with a harelip.

LAWYER/JUDGE JOKES

What is the difference between a wood tick and a lawyer?
A wood tick falls off you when you die.

The airliner was having engine trouble, so the cabin crew told the passengers to take their seats and prepare for an emergency landing, which they all did…except for a lawyer who went around passing out business cards.

A priest and a lawyer died and went to heaven on the same day, and St. Peter showed them both to their rooms. The lawyer's room was extremely large and lavish, but the priest's room was a little ten-by-ten cell with one window and a cot. The priest said, "St. Peter, I have spent my entire life serving God, why do I get a crummy room and the lawyer gets the best room?" St. Peter replied, "Well, we get thousands of priests up here, but this is the first lawyer we've ever had."

What do you have when you've got six lawyers buried up to their necks in sand?
Not enough sand.

A lawyer sent a note to a client:
"Dear Jim: Thought I saw you on the street the other day. Crossed over to say hello, but it wasn't you, so I went back. One-tenth of an hour: $25."

Why won't sharks eat lawyers?
Professional courtesy.

153

Why does New Jersey have so many toxic waste dumps and Washington, D.C., has so many lawyers?

New Jersey got first choice.

The judge said to his dentist: Pull my tooth, the whole tooth, and nothing but the tooth.

A lawyer had just undergone surgery. As he came out of the anesthesia, he said, "Why are all the blinds drawn, Doctor?" "There's a big fire across the street, and we didn't want you to wake up and think the operation was a failure."

A young lawyer meets the devil at a bar association convention and the devil says, "Listen, if you give me your soul and the souls of everyone in your family, I'll make you a full partner in your firm." And the young lawyer says, "So…what's the catch?"

The lawyer is cross-examining the doctor about whether he checked the pulse of the deceased before he signed the death certificate.

"No," he said, "I didn't check his pulse."

"And did you listen for a heartbeat?" said the lawyer.

"No, I did not," said the doctor.

"So," said the lawyer, "when you signed the death certificate, you had not taken steps to make sure he was dead."

And the doctor said, "Well, let me put it this way. The man's brain was in a jar on my desk, but for all I know he could be out practicing law somewhere."

How many lawyers does it take to roof a house?

Depends on how thin you slice them.

This international law firm advertises for a secretary. A golden retriever comes in, and she passes the typing test. In the interview, the personnel manager says, "But how about foreign languages?" And the golden retriever says, "Meow."

Prosecutor: Did you kill the victim?

Defendant: No, I did not.

Prosecutor: Do you know what the penalties are for perjury?

Defendant: Yes, I do. And they're a hell of a lot better than the penalty for murder!

Taking his seat in his chambers, the judge faced the opposing lawyers. "So," he said, "I have been presented by both of you with a bribe." Both lawyers squirmed. "You, attorney Leon, gave me $15,000. And you, attorney Campos, gave me $10,000."

The judge reached into his pocket and pulled out a check. He handed it to Leon. "Now then, I'm returning $5,000, and we're going to decide this case solely on its merits."

Two lawyers went into the restaurant and ordered two drinks. Then they got sandwiches out of their briefcases and started to eat. The waiter said, "Hey, you can't eat your own sandwiches in here!" So the lawyers traded sandwiches.

How was copper wire invented?

Two lawyers were arguing over a penny.

Ninety percent of lawyers give the rest a bad name.

A New York man was forced to take a day off work to appear for a minor traffic summons. He grew increasingly restless as he waited hour after endless hour for his case to be heard. When his name was called late in the afternoon, he stood before the judge only to hear that court would be adjourned, and he would have to return the next day.

"What for?" he snapped at the judge.

His honor, equally irked by a tedious day and the sharp query, roared, "Twenty dollars for contempt of court. That's why!"

Then, noticing the man checking his wallet, the judge relented. "That's all right. You don't have to pay now."

The man replied, "I'm just seeing if I have enough for two more words."

"Are you a lawyer?"

"Yes."

"How much do you charge?"

"A hundred dollars for four questions."

"Isn't that awfully expensive?"

"Yes. What's your fourth question?"

Why is it unethical for lawyers to have sex with their clients?

Because it'd mean being billed twice for essentially the same service.

The defendant knew he didn't have a prayer of beating the murder rap, so he bribed one of the jurors to find him guilty of manslaughter. The jury was out for days before they finally returned a verdict of manslaughter. Afterward the defendant asked, "How come it took you so long?" The juror said, "All the others wanted to acquit."

A lawyer comes to visit his client on death row, and he says, "I have some good news for you." And the client says, "What good news are you talking about? You lost my case, I was convicted of a murder I did not commit, and I've been sentenced to die in the electric chair!" The lawyer says, "Yes, but I got the voltage lowered."

I dated a lawyer for a while, until one time she told me, "Stop and/or I'll slap your face."

The lawyer is painting his house, and a hobo comes around and asks if he can do something to earn a few dollars. The lawyer says, "Sure, take a can of this paint and go around to the back of the house and paint my porch."

The hobo does this and fifteen minutes later comes back and says he's finished. The lawyer says, "Already?"

And the hobo says, "Yeah, but it isn't a Porsche, it's a Mercedes!"

What did the lawyer name his daughter?
   Sue.

ENGINEER JOKES

The mathematician, the physicist, and the engineer were given a red rubber ball and told to find the volume. So the mathematician measured the diameter and evaluated a triple integral. The physicist filled a beaker with water, put the ball in the water, and measured the total displacement. And the engineer looked up the model and serial number in his red-rubber-ball table.

What did the arts graduate say to the engineering graduate?
    Would you like fries with your order, sir?

Three people were going to the guillotine. The first was a lawyer, who was led to the platform, blindfolded, and had his head put on the block. The executioner pulled the lanyard, but nothing happened. To avoid a messy lawsuit, the authorities allowed the lawyer to go free.
    The next man to the guillotine was a priest. They put his head on the block and pulled the lanyard, but nothing happened. The blade didn't come down. They thought it must have been divine intervention, so they let the priest go.
    The third man to the guillotine was an engineer. He waived his right to a blindfold, so they led him to the guillotine and put his head on the block. As he lay there, he said, "Hey, wait. I think I see your problem."

The difference between mechanical engineers and civil engineers is that mechanical engineers build weapons and civil engineers build targets.

The optimist sees a glass that's half full. The pessimist sees a glass that's half empty. An engineer sees a glass that's twice as big as it needs to be.

An engineer walks into his boss' office and his boss is holding a tiny object up to the light. The engineer asks, "What is that you have?"

The boss says, "It looks like plastic but feels like rubber."

The engineer says, "Well, let me have a look at it." So the boss hands it over and the engineer rolls it around between his thumb and his fingers.

"Yes," says the engineer, "It's interesting. It's kind of viscous but also kind of solid. Where'd you get it?"

The boss says, "Out of my nose."

STRICTLY BUSINESS JOKES

The secretary was leaving the office when she saw the CEO standing by a shredder with a piece of paper in his hand. "Listen," said the CEO, "this is a very important document. Can you make this thing work?" The secretary turned the machine on, inserted the paper, and pressed the start button. "Great," said the CEO as his paper disappeared inside the machine. "I just need one copy."

Computers can never completely replace humans. They may become capable of artificial intelligence, but they will never master real stupidity.

A computer is perfectly reliable until the moment you switch it on.

The function of a computer expert is not to be right about more things; it is to be wrong for more sophisticated reasons.

Why is Christmas just like a day at the office?
    You do all the work and the fat guy in the suit gets all the credit.

A programmer is someone who solves a problem you didn't know you had in a way you don't understand.

This customer comes into the computer store. "I'm looking for a mystery adventure game with lots of graphics. You know, something really challenging."
    "Well," replied the clerk, "have you tried Windows '98?"

The crusty old managing partner finally passed away, but his firm kept receiving calls asking to speak with him. "I'm sorry, he's dead," was the standard answer. Finally, the receptionist who fielded the calls began to realize it was always the same voice, so she asked who it was and why he kept calling. The reply was, "I used to be one of his junior associates, and I just like to hear you say it."

A man is flying in a hot air balloon and realizes he is lost. He reduces height and spots a man down below. He lowers the balloon more and shouts, "Excuse me, can you tell me where I am?"

The man below says, "Yes, you're in a hot air balloon, hovering thirty feet above this field."

"You must work in information technology," says the balloonist.

"I do," replies the man. "How did you know?"

"Well," says the balloonist, "everything you have told me is technically correct, but it's of no practical use to anyone."

The man below says, "You must be a corporate manager."

"I am," replies the balloonist. "How did you know?"

"Well," says the man, "you don't know where you are or where you're going, but you expect me to be able to help. You have the same problem you had before we met, but now it's my fault."

IRS/ACCOUNTANT JOKES

The old accountant retired after fifty years, and in the top drawer of his desk they found a note that said: "Debits in the column toward the file cabinet. Credits in the column toward the window."

A man wrote a letter to the IRS: "I have been unable to sleep knowing that I have cheated on my income tax. I understated my taxable income and have enclosed a check for $150. If I still can't sleep, I will send the rest."

A kid swallowed a coin and it got stuck in his throat. His mother yelled for help. A man passing by hit him in the small of the back, and the coin came out.

"I don't know how to thank you, Doctor...," his mother started.

"I'm not a doctor," the man replied, "I'm from the IRS."

Two accountants are in a bank when armed robbers burst in. While several of the robbers take the money from the tellers, others line up the customers, including the accountants, and proceed to take their wallets, watches, etc. While this is going on, the first accountant jams something into the second accountant's hand. Without looking down, the second accountant whispers, "What is this?" To which the first accountant replies, "It's that $50 I owe you."

ECONOMIST JOKES

An economist is an expert who will know tomorrow why the things he predicted yesterday did not happen today.

A woman hears from her doctor that she has only half a year to live. The doctor advises her to marry an economist and to live in South Dakota. The woman asks, "Will this cure my illness?"

The doctor answers, "No, but the half year will seem pretty long."

A mathematician, an accountant, and an economist apply for the same job. The interviewer calls in the mathematician and asks, "What does two plus two equal?" The mathematician replies, "Four." The interviewer asks, "Four exactly?" The mathematician looks at the interviewer incredulously and says, "Yes, four exactly."

Then the interviewer calls in the accountant and asks the same question: "What does two plus two equal?" The accountant says, "On average, four—give or take 10 percent—but on average, four."

Then the interviewer calls in the economist and poses the same question: "What does two plus two equal?" The economist gets up, locks the door, closes the shade, sits down next to the interviewer, and says, "What do you want it to equal?"

Why was astrology invented?

So economics could be an accurate science.

Three econometricians went out hunting and came across a large deer. The first econometrician fired but missed by a meter to the left. The second econometrician fired but missed by a meter to the right. The third econometrician didn't fire but shouted in triumph, "We got it! We got it!"

An economist is someone who didn't have enough personality to become an accountant.

What's the difference between an economist and a confused old man with Alzheimer's?
    The economist is the one with the calculator.

A party of economists was climbing in the Alps. After several hours they became hopelessly lost. One of them studied the map for some time, turning it up and down, sighting on distant landmarks, consulting his compass and the sun. Finally he said,"Okay, see that big mountain over there?"
    The others agreed. "Well, according to the map, we're standing on top of it."

Economists have forecast nine out of the last five recessions.

DOCTOR/PSYCHIATRIST JOKES

Doctor: What seems to be the matter?

Patient: I have a sore throat, Doctor. I ache, I have a fever.

Doctor: Sounds like some kind of virus.

Patient: Everyone in the office has it.

Doctor: Well then, maybe it's a staff infection.

"I have terrible news, Mr. Larson. You have cancer and you have Alzheimer's."

"Well, Doctor, at least I don't have cancer."

"Doctor, I feel like a pair of curtains."

"Come now, pull yourself together."

"Doctor, there is an invisible man in your waiting room."

"Tell him I can't see him now."

"Doctor, you told me I have a month to live and then you sent me a bill for $1,000! I can't pay that before the end of the month!"

"Okay, you have six months to live."

"Doctor, am I going to die?"

"That's the last thing you're going to do."

"Doctor, my fingers hurt. Do you think I should file my nails?"

"No, just throw them away."

Patient: How much to have this tooth pulled?
    Dentist: Ninety dollars.
    Patient: Ninety dollars for just a few minutes' work?
    Dentist: I can do it slower if you like.

A man consults a therapist and states, "Doc, I'm suicidal. What should I do?"
    The doctor replies, "Pay in advance."

"Mrs. Larson, you're not going deaf in your left ear. You
    seem to have a suppository stuck in there!"
    "Well, now I know what happened to my hearing aid."

"Doctor, I don't know what's wrong with me, but I hurt all over. If I touch my shoulder here, it hurts, and if I touch my leg here, it hurts, and if I touch my head here, it hurts, and if I touch my foot here, it hurts."
    "I believe you've broken your finger."

"What's wrong, Doctor? You look puzzled."
    "I can't figure out exactly what's wrong with you. I think it's the result of heavy drinking."
    "Well then, I'll just come back when you're sober."

The doctor calls up the patient and says, "I have some bad news and some worse news. The bad news is that you have only twenty-four hours left to live." And the patient says, "That is very bad news. What could be worse than that?" And the doctor says, "I've been trying to reach you since yesterday."

Patient: Doctor, every time I sneeze, I have an orgasm.

Doctor: Are you taking anything for it?

Patient: Ground pepper!

Pharmacist: Sir, pardon me for asking, but every week you come in here to my drugstore and buy two dozen condoms.

Customer: Yes?

Pharmacist: It's none of my business, but how on earth do you use that many condoms a week?

Customer: I feed them to my poodle and now when she poops, she poops in little plastic bags.

A ninety-year-old man went to his doctor and said, "Doctor, my wife, who is eighteen, is expecting a baby."

The doctor said, "Let me tell you a story. A man went hunting, but instead of his gun, he picked up an umbrella by mistake. And when a bear suddenly charged at him, he pointed his umbrella at the bear, shot at it, and killed it on the spot."

"Impossible. Somebody else must have shot that bear."

"Exactly my point."

A man accidentally cut off all his fingers with a power saw. When he got to the hospital, the doctor said, "Thank goodness for microsurgery. Give me the fingers and I'll sew them back on."

The man said, "I haven't got the fingers. I couldn't pick them up."

PROFESSIONALLY SPEAKING

Woman: So give it to me straight, Doctor. I want to know the truth.

Doctor: Very well. Your husband is in terrible shape, and if you want him to live, you're going to have to make sure he's well fed and comfortable and happy at all times, and you're going to have to make love to him three times a day.

Woman: Three times a day?

Doctor: Three times a day.

Husband: So what'd the doctor say?

Woman: He says you're going to die.

A woman goes to the doctor and says, "Doctor, Doctor, you have to help me. Every time I go to the bathroom, dimes come out!"

The doctor tells her to relax, go home, rest with her feet up, and come back in a week.

A week later the woman returns and says, "Doctor, Doctor, it's gotten worse! Every time I go to the bathroom, quarters come out! What's wrong with me?" Again the doctor tells her to relax, go home, rest with her feet up, and come back in a week.

Another week passes. The woman returns and yells, "Doctor, Doctor, I'm still not getting better! Every time I go to the bathroom, half-dollars come out! What the heck is wrong with me?"

The doctor says, "Relax, relax, you're just going through your change."

Did you hear the one about the two carrots who are riding in a car? They get into a terrible accident, and they're rushed to the hospital. One of the carrots just has some scrapes and bruises, but the other is rushed to the operating room.

Hours later, the doctor comes out and says, "I have some good news and some bad news. The good news is that your friend is going to live. The bad news is that he's going to be a vegetable for the rest of his life."

"What happened to you, Mr. Peebles? You look awful."

"Well, Doctor, you told me to take this medicine for three days and then skip a day, and all that skipping wore me out."

The old family physician took his son into partnership after the son got his M.D. The old doctor then went off on a two-week vacation, his first in years. When he got home, he asked his son if there'd been any problems at the clinic. The son said no, everything went well. "In fact," he said, "you know that rich old widow, Mrs. Ferguson? I cured her of her chronic indigestion."

"Well, that's fine," said the old doctor. "Mrs. Ferguson's indigestion is what put you through medical school."

Patient: Say, Doctor? What was wrong with that nun who just came running out of your office? She looked terribly pale.

Doctor: Well, I examined her and told her she was pregnant.

Patient: Is she?

Doctor: No, but it sure as hell cured her hiccups!

Patient: Nurse, I keep seeing spots in front of my eyes.
Nurse: Have you ever seen a doctor?
Patient: No, just spots.

So, this man walks into the pharmacy and says, "Have you got cotton balls?"
The pharmacist says, "What is this, a joke?"

The man came to see the doctor about his constant fatigue and the doctor said, "I'm afraid you're going to have to give up sex."
The man said, "But I'm a young guy. I'm in the prime of my life. How can I just give up sex?"
"Well," the doctor said, "you do what everyone does. You get married and you taper off gradually."

Doctor! Something's wrong! I'm shrinking!
Take it easy, sir. You'll just have to be a little patient.

The doctor calls up the patient and says, "I've got some good news and some bad news for you." And the patient says, "What's the good news, Doctor?" And the doctor says, "They're going to name a disease after you."

Woman: Doctor, for the last eight months, my husband has thought that he's a lawn mower.
Doctor: That's terrible. Why didn't you bring him in sooner?
Woman: Because the neighbor just returned him this morning.

Pharmacist: May I help you, sir?

Customer: Yes...I, uh...well, this is sort of embarrassing, but I'm going out on a date tonight, and you know, I need some...

Pharmacist: You need some protection.

Customer: Right.

Pharmacist: Small, medium, or large?

Customer: Uhhhh. Medium, I guess.

Pharmacist: Okay, that'll be $2.35 including tax.

Customer: Tacks!! I thought they stayed on by themselves!

A man was very unhappy that he had no romance in his life whatsoever. So, he went to a Chinese sex therapist, Dr. Chang, who looked at him and said, "Okay, take off all your crose." Which the man did.

"Now, get down and crawl reery fass to the other side of room." Which the man did. "Okay, now crawl reery fass to me." Which the man did. Dr. Chang said, "Your probrem velly bad. You haf Ed Zachary Disease." The man said, "What is Ed Zachary Disease?"

"It when your face rook Ed Zachary rike your ass."

Doctor: What's wrong with your brother?

Boy: He thinks he's a chicken.

Doctor: Really? How long has he thought this?

Boy: Three years.

Doctor: Three years!

Boy: We would've brought him in sooner, but we needed the eggs.

A woman went to a dentist to have a tooth pulled and there was instant electricity between the two. They made love right there in his office. She came back week after week after week and they made love over and over and over again. Until one day he told her they'd have to end the affair, as beautiful as it was, because she only had one tooth left.

There's so much more that medical science knows now than it ever used to. When my wife went in for her sonogram, she found out that the baby is a lesbian.

"Hello? Is this the state mental hospital?"
    "Yes, it is."
    "Can I speak to Mr. Russell in room twenty-seven?"
    "One moment and I'll connect you… (*pause*) I'm sorry, Mr. Russell is not answering."
    "Good. That means I must have really escaped."

A man is feeling poorly, so he goes to his doctor. After numerous tests the doc says, "I'm sorry, but you have an incurable condition and there is nothing more I can do for you." The man pleads with the doctor to suggest anything he might do to improve his condition, and the doctor then suggests that he go to the spa and take a daily mud bath. "Is there any hope of a cure?" the man asks. "No," says the doctor, "but it will help you get used to dirt."

Patient: I'm feeling terrible. Am I dying?

Doctor: I'll have to examine you. Hmm…hmmm…I'm afraid I have some bad news. You're dying and you don't have much time.

Patient: Oh no! How long have I got?

Doctor: Ten…

Patient: Ten? Ten what?

Doctor: Nine…

Patient: Nine? Nine what—months? weeks? what?!

Doctor: Eight…seven…six…

A painter got a call from the gallery that was showing his work. The gallery owner said, "I have good news and bad news. A fellow came in this morning and asked if your work is the kind that would increase in value after the artist's death. I said yes, and he bought all fifteen paintings. The bad news is that he's your doctor."

A guy goes to the doctor, and the doctor tells him he only has a day to live. He goes home to tell his wife, who asks him what he wants to do with his final hours. Of course he wants to spend them having sex. They have great sex all night long.

Finally, about two a.m., the wife says she's tired and wants to go to sleep. He says, "Oh, come on, can't we do it just one more time?" And she says, "Look, I've got to get up in the morning—you don't!"

A man walks into the psychiatrist's office with a cucumber up his nose, a carrot in his left ear, and a banana in his right ear. He says, "What's the matter with me?"

The psychiatrist says, "You're not eating properly."

Doctor: Sir, how did you happen to break your leg?

Patient: Well, Doctor, it was like this. Twenty-five years ago, I was on the road and it got dark and…

Doctor: Never mind that. Tell me how you broke your leg this morning.

Patient: Well, twenty-five years ago, I was on the road and it got dark, and I needed a place to stay. There was only this one farmhouse near, so I knocked on the door and the farmer answered. I told him my situation, and he said, "Well, you can stay here, but you'll have to share a room with my beautiful daughter." I said that would be okay, and I went up and crawled into bed. She was already asleep, and that night, right after I'd gone to sleep, she woke me up and asked me if there was anything I wanted. I said no, everything was fine. She said, "Are you sure?" I said, "I'm sure." She said, "Isn't there *anything* I can do for you?" I said, "I reckon not."

Doctor: What does this have to do with your broken leg?

Patient: Well, this morning, it dawned on me what she meant by that, and I fell off the roof!

Patient: Doctor, you've got to help me. Some mornings I wake up and think I'm Donald Duck, other mornings I think I'm Mickey Mouse.

Doctor: Hmm, and how long have you been having these Disney spells?

174

When the X-ray specialist married one of his patients, everybody wondered what he saw in her.

Never go to a doctor whose office plants have died.

Doctor, I think I'm suffering from memory loss.
 Have you ever had it before?

How did it go at the doctor's today, honey?
 The doctor told me I have to take medication every day for the rest of my life.
 What's so terrible about that?
 He only gave me four pills.

Why do surgeons wear masks during operations?
 So they can't be identified.

One reason surgeons are paid more than auto mechanics is that auto mechanics don't have to repair the engine while it's running.

My doctor tried kidnapping for a while, but nobody could read the ransom notes.

Doctor: Nurse, how is that little girl doing who swallowed ten quarters last night?
 Nurse: No change yet.

I was depressed, Doctor, so I tried to kill myself by taking 1,000 aspirin.

What happened?

Well, after the first two I felt better.

Am I going to be okay, doctor?

Sir, there's nothing to worry about, the operation is quite routine and not at all complicated.

Good. I hope you remember that when you're writing up the bill.

Psychiatrist: Mr. Phelps, I can say with confidence that after fifteen years of psychotherapy you are cured.

Patient: Well, that's good, I guess. But on the other hand, fifteen years ago I was God. Now I'm nobody.

I asked my doctor if I should have a vasectomy. He said to leave a sleeping dog lie.

Patient: Doctor, I have this terrible problem. I think I'm a dog. I walk around on all fours, I keep barking in the middle of the night and I eat dog food.

Doctor: Very interesting. Lie down on the couch, please.

Patient: I'm not allowed on the couch.

Visitor: I'm here to see a friend who was admitted to the hospital this morning. He was run over by a steamroller.

Nurse: He's in Room 105, 106, 107, 108, and 109.

Father: I'm dying.

Son: Yes, Dad.

Father: Somehow I never expected this to happen to me.

Son: I know, Dad.

Father: I'm not ready to go.

Son: Where do you want to be buried, Dad?

Father: Surprise me.

A man is walking by an insane asylum and hears all the residents chanting, "Thirteen! Thirteen! Thirteen!" He's very curious about all this, so he finds a hole in the fence, looks in and someone pokes him in the eye with a sharp stick. Everyone in the asylum starts chanting "Fourteen! Fourteen! Fourteen!"

Psychoanalysis is easier for a man, because when it's time to go back to childhood, he is already there.

After twelve years of analysis, I finally was able to get in touch with my emotions and break down and cry.

What happened?

One day, my analyst looked at me and said, "*No hablo inglés.*"

Doctor: You are in perfect health. You'll live to be at least 65.

Patient: But Doctor, I am 65!

Doctor: See? What did I tell you?

Patient: Doctor! I can't feel my legs!

Doctor: That's because we had to amputate your arms.

A guy goes into a doctor's office wearing nothing but a piece of cling film around his waist. The doctor says, "I can clearly see you're nuts."

"Hello, doctor?"

"Yes?"

"My wife is pregnant, and her contractions are only two minutes apart!"

"Is this her first child?"

"No, this is her husband!"

We've got bad news and we have good news, Mrs. Olson. The bad news is that we've amputated the wrong leg. The good news is that your bad leg is getting better.

We've got bad news and we have good news, Mrs. Olson. The bad news is that we've had to amputate the other leg, too. The good news is that the lady in the next room made a very good offer on your shoes.

COP JOKES

A juggler, driving to his next performance, is stopped by the police.

"What are those knives doing in your car?" asks the officer.

"I juggle them in my act," says the juggler

"Oh yeah?" says the cop. "Let's see you do it." So the juggler starts tossing and juggling the knives.

A guy driving by sees this and says, "Wow, am I glad I quit drinking. Look at the test they're making you do now!"

The state trooper is driving down the highway when he sees a truck driver pull over, walk to the side of his truck with a tire jack, bang on the side of the truck several times, and then drive away. Two miles down the road he does the same thing. Another two miles, same thing. The trooper pulls the truck over and asks the truck driver to explain. And the driver says, "The load limit is ten tons, and I'm carrying fifteen tons of parakeets, so I've got to keep some of them flying around."

The police officer sees a car weaving back and forth down the highway, and he takes off after it. He pulls up alongside and sees the driver is a little old lady, and she's knitting as she drives. He can't believe it, and he yells at her, "Pull over! Pull over!"

And she yells, "No, it's a scarf!"

All the toilet seats were stolen from police headquarters. The police have nothing to go on.

The town cop was parked outside a bar at midnight, watching for drunk drivers, when he saw a man stumble out the door, trip over the curb, try thirty cars before opening the door to his own, and fall asleep on the front seat. One by one the drivers of the other cars drive off, and finally the guy wakes up, starts his car, and pulls out of the parking lot. The cop pulls him over and gives him a Breathalyzer test. The results shows a 0.0 blood-alcohol level, and the cop is puzzled. He asks, "How can that be?" The guy says, "Well, tonight was my turn to be the decoy."

This cop pulled a guy over and said, "Sir, I need you to breathe into this Breathalyzer for me."

"I can't do that. I'm an asthmatic. If I do that, I'll have a really big asthma attack."

"Okay. Then I need you to come down to the station with me and we'll have to do some blood work."

"I can't do that, either. I'm a hemophiliac. If I do that, I'll bleed to death."

"Okay. Then I need a urine sample from you."

"I can't do that, either. I'm a diabetic. If I do that, my sugar will get really low."

"Okay. Then I need you to step out of the car and walk this white line."

"I can't do that, either."

The cop said, "Why not?"

The guy said, "Because I'm drunk."

This old rancher in Montana hates wearing a seat belt. One day he's driving on the highway with his wife and sees a state patrol car behind him. He says to his wife, "Quick, take the wheel! I gotta put my seat belt on!" So she does, and right then the patrolman pulls them over. He walks up to the car and says to the rancher, "Say, I noticed you weren't wearing your seat belt."

The rancher says, "I was too, but you don't have to take my word for it. My wife here is a good Christian woman, ask her. She'll tell you the truth. She doesn't lie about anything."

The cop says to the wife, "So? How about it, ma'am?" And the wife says, "I've been married to Buck for twenty years, officer, and one thing I've learned in all that time is this: You never argue with him when he's drunk."

Cop pulling a woman over: Let me see your driver's license, lady.

Woman: I wish you people would get it together. One day you take away my license and the next day you ask me to show it.

MUSICIAN JOKES

A banjo is like an artillery shell—by the time you hear it, it's too late.

What's the difference between a banjo and a lawnmower?
    You can tune a lawnmower.

What's the difference between a banjo and a vacuum cleaner?
    You have to plug in a vacuum cleaner before it sucks.

Do you know the definition for perfect pitch?
    When you throw the banjo into the dumpster and it lands right on the accordion.

What's the difference between an accordion and an onion?
    No one cries when you cut up an accordion.

Definition of an optimist
    • An accordion player with a pager.
    • A choir director with a mortgage.

Hey, buddy. How late does the band play?
    Oh, about half a beat behind the drummer.

What do you call a guy who hangs out with musicians?
    A drummer.

How do you get a drummer out of your house?
    Pay him for the pizza.

182

Why do drummers leave their sticks on the dashboard when they park?
So they can use the handicapped zones.

How can you tell that there's a drummer at your front door?
Gradually, the knocking gets faster and faster.

Why are orchestra intermissions limited to 20 minutes?
So you don't have to retrain the drummers.

What's the difference between a drummer and a drum machine?
With a drum machine you only have to punch the information in once.

What's the difference between drummers and government bonds?
Government bonds eventually mature and earn money.

How can you tell when the drum riser is level?
Drool comes out of both sides of the drummer's mouth.

What's the last thing a drummer says before he's out of a band?
"Hey guys, why don't we try one of my songs?"

Why do bands have bass players?
To translate for the drummer.

One day the bass player hid one of the drummer's sticks. The drummer said, "Finally! After all these years, I'm a conductor!"

The gig's going really well. I mean really well. The crowd is going wild—people are dancing, yelling, and applauding loudly after every song, and the house is packed. There's someone who looks to be a talent agent in the back. The whole band is having a great night, hitting every groove, pulling off every little detail to make it right.

The guitarist thinks, "We're going to be famous. I'm going to be famous! Everyone's going to know my name. I'm going to have a lot of sex."

The drummer thinks, "We're going to be rich. So rich. I'm going to buy a ton of gear."

The singer/rhythm guitarist thinks, "This is wonderful. I can finally support my designer drug habit."

The bassist thinks, "G - D - C - D - G."

Did you hear about the bassist who was so out of tune his section noticed?

A double bass player arrived a few minutes late for the first rehearsal of the local choral society's annual performance of Handel's Messiah.

He picked up his instrument and bow, and turned his attention to the conductor. The conductor asked, "Would you like a moment to tune?"

The bass player replied with some surprise, "Why? Isn't it the same as last year?"

Why does a violinist have a handkerchief under his chin when he plays?

Because there's no spit valve.

I recommend that you don't buy a Stradivarius. He stopped making parts for them.

Why are violins smaller than violas?

They're really the same size, but violinists have bigger heads.

A policeman went up to a street musician and asked, "Excuse me, sir, do you have a license to play that violin in the street?"

And the violinist answered, "Well, actually, no."

"In that case I'm going to have to ask you to accompany me."

"Of course, officer. What would you like to sing?"

Why are viola jokes so short?

So violinists can understand them.

How do you tell the difference between a violinist and a dog?

The dog knows when to stop scratching.

What do a viola and a lawsuit have in common?

Everyone's happy when the case is closed.

How do you get two viola players to play in perfect unison?

Shoot one of them.

Why do so many people take an instant dislike to the viola?
    It saves time.

What's the difference between the first and last desk of a viola section?
    Half a measure and a semi-tone.

Did you hear about the violist who bragged that he could play 32nd notes?
    The rest of the orchestra didn't believe him, so he proved it by playing one.

How can you tell if a viola is out of tune?
    The bow is moving.

What's the difference between a cello and a viola?
    A cello burns longer.

A viola player came home late at night to find police cars and fire trucks outside his house. The chief of police intercepted him.
    "I'm afraid I have terrible news for you. While you were out, the conductor came to your house, killed your family and burned your house down."
    The viola player was stunned. "You're kidding! The conductor came to my house?"

What's the difference between a viola and a coffin?
    The coffin has the dead person on the inside.

Did you hear about the violist who dreamed she was playing in the pit for *The Nutcracker*, and she woke up and found out that she was?

During a concert, a fight broke out between the oboe player and the viola player. At the intermission, the orchestra leader went to investigate.

"He broke my reed," said the oboe player.

"He undid two of my strings," countered the viola player, "and he won't tell me which ones."

What's the definition of a quarter tone?

Two oboes playing in unison.

What's the difference between a saxophone and a lawn mower?

• Lawn mowers sound better in small ensembles.

• The neighbors are upset if you borrow a lawnmower and don't return it.

• The grip.

What's the difference between a baritone sax and a chain saw?

Vibrato.

How can you tell which kid on a playground is the child of a trombonist?

He doesn't know how to use the slide, and he can't swing.

A girl went out on a date with a trumpet player, and when she came back her roommate asked, "Well, how was it? Did his embouchure make him a great kisser?"

"Nah," the first girl replied. "That dry, tight, tiny pinched up mouth; it was no fun at all."

The next night she went out with a tuba player, and when she came back her roommate asked, "Well, was he a good kisser?"

"Ugh!" the first girl exclaimed. "Those huge, rubbery, blubbery, slobbering lips! Oh, it was just gross!"

The next night she went out with a French horn player, and when she came back her roommate asked, "Well, how was his kissing?"

"Well," the first girl replied, "his kissing was just so-so; but I loved the way he held me!"

Why can't a gorilla play trumpet?
He's too sensitive.

What's a tuba for?
1 ½" by 3 ½" unless you request "full cut."

What is the difference between a dead trombone player lying in the road and a dead squirrel lying in the road?
The squirrel might have been on his way to a job.

What is the dynamic range of the bass trombone?
On or off.

What do you get when you drop a piano down a mine shaft?

A-flat minor.

Pianist to singer: "You keep your hands off my piano and I'll keep my hands off your throat."

The doorbell rang, and the lady of the house discovered a workman, complete with tool chest, on the front porch.

"Madam," he announced, "I'm the piano tuner." The lady exclaimed, "Why, I didn't send for a piano tuner." The man replied, "I know, but your neighbors did."

A pianist gave a solo recital. When it was over, he got a big ovation, and a woman in the front row stood up and shouted, "Play it again! Play it again!" He stepped forward and bowed. She yelled, "Play it again until you get it right!"

I play piano just like Frederic Chopin—with both hands.

Why couldn't Mozart find his teacher?

Because he was Haydn.

Why did Beethoven kill his chicken? It kept saying "Bach, Bach, Bach..."

They laughed when I sat down at the piano. I forgot to bring a stool.

How do you get to the Catskills?

Stop practicing.

189

Two musicians are walking down the street, and one says to the other, "Who was that piccolo I saw you with last night?"

The other replies, "That was no piccolo, that was my fife."

I'm in a three-piece band. We only know three pieces.

I play in a small quartet. There's only three of us.

How do you make a bandstand?
Take away their chairs.

So a seven-year-old kid says to his dad, "When I grow up, I want to be a musician."

And the dad says, "I'm sorry—you can't have it both ways."

St. Peter's checking IDs. He asks a man, "What did you do on Earth?"

The man says, "I was a doctor."

St. Peter says, "Ok, go right through those pearly gates. Next! What did you do on Earth?"

"I was a school teacher."

"Go right through those pearly gates. Next! And what did you do on Earth?"

"I was a musician."

"Go around the side, up the freight elevator, through the kitchen..."

The organ is the instrument of worship, for in its sounding we sense the majesty of God and in its ending we know the grace of God.

Two out-of-work Jewish musicians are sitting on a park bench in Brooklyn.

The first one says, "Oy!"

The other one says, "I'm hip."

What do you call a musician without a girlfriend?

Homeless.

What's the difference between a musician and a fourteen-inch pizza?

The pizza can feed a family of four.

How do you get a guitar player to turn down the volume?

Put sheet music in front of him.

How does a guitar player make a million dollars?

He starts out with seven million.

Either heaven or hell will have continuous background music. Which one you think it will be tells a lot about you.

The other day I saw one of those pop singers with an exposed belly but no navel. It's either a show-biz gimmick or the ultimate rejection of mother.

I was a musical prodigy. At three I composed an opera. At four I wrote a minuet. At five I wrote a complete symphony. And at five thirty, as usual, I went down and had a cup of tea.

My friend was trying to write a drinking song but he couldn't get past the first few bars.

191

To be a real folk-singer you have to collect the songs straight from the horse's mouth. The way to do this is to go to a village and find the oldest inhabitant and ask him to sing you the songs his mother taught him. You'll probably find out that he's deaf, and if he isn't deaf he can't sing, and if he can sing he doesn't want to, and by the time you've persuaded him and he does sing, you won't understand a word of what he's singing about. This is how folk songs have been passed down from generation to generation.

A jazz musician dies and goes to heaven. He is told "Hey man, welcome! You have been elected to the Jazz All-Stars of Heaven—right up there with Satchmo, Miles, Django, all the greats. We have a gig tonight. Only one problem—God's got this girlfriend who's a singer..."

Why do bagpipers always walk when they play?
    To get away from the noise.

There was a young Scottish boy called Angus who decided to try life in Australia. He found an apartment in a small block and settled in.
    After a week or two, his mother called from Aberdeen to see how her son was doing in his new life. "I'm fine," Angus said. "But there are some really strange people living in these apartments. The woman next door cried all night long, and the guy upstairs bangs his foot on the floor all the time."
    "Well, ma laddie," says his mother, "I suggest you don't associate with people like that."
    "Oh," says Angus, "I don't, Mam, I stay inside my apartment all day and night, playing my bagpipes."

Why do high school choruses travel so often?
    To keep would-be assassins guessing.

How do you know you have a singer at your front door?
    Can't find the key; doesn't know when to come in.

Twelve tenors and a baritone were climbing Mount Everest
and they fell down into the crevasse. All of them managed to
hang on to the rope, but it was clear that the rope couldn't
hold them all. They decided one man would have to let go.
The baritone said, "Okay, I'm only a baritone. There are so
many baritones and so few tenors. The music world cannot
bear to lose you, so I'll sacrifice myself to save your lives."
And the tenors all applauded and fell to their deaths.

What's the difference between a soprano and the PLO?
    You can negotiate with the PLO.

What's the difference between a soprano and a Rottweiler?
    Jewelry.

What's the difference between a Wagnerian soprano and a
Wagnerian tenor?
    About 10 pounds.

How do you tell if a Wagnerian soprano is dead?
    The horses seem very relieved.

What's the difference between an alto and a tenor?
    Tenors don't have hair on their backs.

First woman: What did you hear at the opera yesterday?
    Second woman: Oh, lots of things. The Williamses are going to Hawaii this winter. Elsa is pregnant again…

What do you get when you play country music backwards?
    You get your wife back, your dog back, your car back…

What do you get when you play New Age music backwards?
    New Age music.

What does it say on a blues singer's tombstone?
    "I didn't wake up this morning…"

What's the difference between a puppy and a singer-songwriter?
    Eventually the puppy stops whining.

A new conductor was at his first rehearsal. It was not going well. He was as wary of the musicians as they were of him. As he left the rehearsal room, the timpanist sounded a rude little "bong." The angry conductor turned and said, "All right! Who did that?"

How many musician jokes are there?
    Just one—all the rest are true.

AND A FEW MORE JOB JOKES

A statistician is someone who is good with numbers but lacks the personality to be an accountant. An accountant is someone who solves a problem you didn't know you had in a way you don't understand. A psychologist is a man who, when a beautiful woman enters the room, watches everyone else. A professor is someone who talks in someone else's sleep. A schoolteacher is a woman who used to think she liked small children. A consultant is someone who takes the watch off your wrist and tells you the time.

A teacher was telling her third-grade class that they needed to bring in a couple dollars to get a copy of the class picture. "This is going to mean so much to you in thirty years," she said. "You'll look at it and you'll say, there's my friend Julie, she's a lawyer now, and there's my friend Jim…" A voice from the back of the room interrupted, "And there's my teacher, she's dead."

Two cowboys are riding across the prairie and they come across an Indian lying down with his ear on the ground. They get off their horses and ask him what he's doing. He says, "Two wagons, four horses, two men, two women, one small child, one cow, two goats, and one large brown dog." They say, "Wow, you can tell all of that by listening to the ground?!" He says, "No, they ran over me half an hour ago."

Why was the archeologist depressed?
His career was in ruins.

Did you hear that archeologists just recently identified the cause of the Dark Ages?

It was most definitely the Y1K problem.

Did you hear about the flasher who was thinking of retiring?

He decided to stick it out for one more year.

Four people were riding in a train coach. A woman and her beautiful nineteen-year-old daughter were on one side, and facing them were the army general and his escort, an army private. The train enters a tunnel, and the cabin becomes dark. A kiss is heard, followed by a slap. The mother thinks, "That young man stole a kiss from my daughter, and she rightfully slapped him." The daughter thinks, "That young man tried to kiss me and kissed my mother by mistake and got slapped." The general thinks, "That young man stole a kiss, and I got slapped by mistake." The private thinks, "I'm pretty smart. I kiss the back of my hand and get to hit the general."

The old retired general goes into the base hospital for his annual physical. "Any complaints about your physical condition?" the doctor asks. "My sex life isn't as good as it used to be," complains the general. "Really, General, when was the last time you had sexual relations?" asks the doctor. "1958!" says the general. "Well, no wonder," says the doctor, "that's an awfully long time ago and you're an old man!" The general, angry, replies, "Whaddya mean, it's only a little after 2100 right now!"

A biologist, an engineer, and a mathematician were sitting outside an empty house. They saw two people go in, and a while later, three people came out. The engineer said, "Our initial count must have been wrong." The biologist said, "They must have reproduced." The mathematician said, "Now, if one person goes back into the house, it will be completely empty!"

Teacher: Class, it's an interesting linguistic fact that, in English, a double negative forms a positive. In some languages though, such as Russian, a double negative is still a negative. However, there is no language in which a double positive can form a negative.
  Student: Yeah, right.

The NYPD, the FBI, and the CIA have engaged for years in serious competition to determine which organization is the most deft apprehender of criminals. The president, wanting to resolve the question once and for all, releases a rabbit into a forest and challenges each organization to utilize its best methods to bring the rabbit in to him.
  The CIA goes in. They place animal informants throughout the forest. They place hidden microphones on all of the trees and motion detectors behind each rock. After three months of extensive investigations, they conclude that rabbits do not exist.
  The FBI goes in. After two weeks with no leads, they burn the forest, killing everything in it, including the rabbit, and they make no apologies—the rabbit had it coming.
  The NYPD goes in. A mere two hours later they come out leading a badly beaten bear by the ear. The bear is yelling: "Okay, okay, I'm a rabbit, I'm a rabbit."

The human cannonball decided he was too old to go on being shot across the circus arena and into a net night after night. So he went to the circus owner and told him he was going to retire. The owner cried, "But you can't! Where am I going to find a man of your caliber?"

This man got a job with the county highway department painting lines down the center of the highway. The supervisor told him he was expected to paint two miles of highway a day, and the man started work the next day. The first day the man painted four miles. The supervisor thought, "Great." The next day the man only painted two miles but the supervisor thought, "Well, it's good enough." But the third day the man only painted one mile and the boss went out to talk to him. He said, "Is there a problem? An injury? Some reason you keep painting less and less highway?" The man said, "Well, I keep getting farther and farther from the bucket."

A sadistic drill sergeant runs his platoon of recruits all over the camp in the hot sun with heavy packs on. As they stand there, exhausted, he puts his face right up to one recruit's face and says, "I'll bet you're wishing I would die so you could come and urinate on my grave, aren't you?"

And the recruit says, "No, sir! When I get out of the army I'm never gonna stand in another line again."

A manager is a person who thinks that nine women ought to be able to produce a child in one month.

A consultant is a man who knows 147 ways to make love, but doesn't know any women.

My boss is so mean, if you get in two minutes late he fines you and if you get in two minutes early he charges you rent.

What to say if you get caught sleeping in your work cubicle:
• It's okay: I'm still billing the client.
• Do you discriminate against people who practice yoga?"
• I wasn't sleeping. I was trying to pick up a contact lens without using my hands.

Useful Phrases for the Workplace:
• Thank you. We're all refreshed and challenged by your unique point of view.
• The fact that no one understands you doesn't mean you're an artist.
• You are validating my inherent mistrust of strangers.
• I will always cherish the initial misconceptions I had about you.
• What am I? Flypaper for freaks!?
• I'm not being rude. You're just insignificant.
• I'll try being nicer if you'll try being smarter.

I earned my sergeant's stripes the hard way. The really hard way: I started out as a lieutenant.

My only regret was that I had but one life to give for my country. If I'd had two, I would have felt a lot safer.

Sergeant: Private!

Private: Yes, sir.

Sergeant: You failed to show up for camouflage class yesterday.

Private: How do you know that, sir?

Copy-editing is a very stressful line of work for women. Every time one of us misses a period, we get really nervous.

For every philosopher, there exists an equal and opposite philosopher.

I got an A in philosophy last semester by proving that my professor doesn't exist.

The philosopher went out on his first date with a woman and took her to a restaurant. They sat quietly for awhile and he finally says, "Do you like philosophy?"

She says, "No."

He says. "Do you have a brother?"

"No."

He says, "If you had a brother, do you think he'd like philosophy?"

OLE & LENA JOKES

Ole came home from work one day and found Lena sitting on the edge of the bed, naked. He asked her, "Lena, why are you sitting there without any clothes on?" And Lena said, "I don't have no clothes to wear." Ole said, "Don't be silly—you got lots of clothes." And he went over to the closet, flung open the door, and said, "Lena, look—here's a blue dress, here's a yellow dress, here's Sven, here's a flowered dress..."

Ole and Sven go on a fishing trip to Canada and come back with only three fish. Sven says, "The way I figger it, Ole, each of them fish cost us $400."

Ole says, "Well, at dat price it's a good ting we didn't catch any more of 'em than we did."

Ole: I need to buy some boards there, Sven.
   Sven: How long you want 'em, Ole?
   Ole: Long time. I'm building a house, ya know.

Lena was competing in the Sons of Norway swim meet. She came in last in the hundred-yard breast stroke, and she said to the judges, "Oh say, I don't vant to complain, but I tink those other two girls ver using dere arms!"

Ole: Say, I went and bought Lena a piano for her birthday and then about a week later I traded it in for a clarinet, because you know, with a clarinet, you can't sing.

Sven and Ole went out duck hunting. They worked at it for a couple hours and finally Sven says, "I wonder why aren't we getting any ducks, Ole?"

"I don't know," says Ole. "I wonder if we're throwing the dog high enough."

Did you hear about Ole's nephew Torvald who won the gold medal at the Olympics? He had it bronzed.

Ole got a car phone and on his way home on the freeway, he calls up Lena and says, "Oh, Lena, I'm calling you from the freeway on my new car phone." And Lena says, "Be careful, Ole, because on the radio they say that some nut is driving the wrong way on the freeway." And Ole says, "One nut—heck, there are hundreds of them!"

Sven and Ole are walking home from the tavern late at night, and they head down the railroad tracks. Sven says, "This is the longest flight of stairs I ever climbed in my life." And Ole says, "Yeah, it's not the stairs that bother me, it's these low railings."

Ole: Sven, how many Swedes does it take to grease a combine?
　　Sven: I don't know, Ole.
　　Ole: Only two if you run them through real slow.

Sven: So, Ole—I see you got a sign up that says "Boat for Sale." But you don't own a boat. All you got is your old John Deere tractor and your combine.
　　Ole: Yup, and they're boat for sale.

Ole was fishing with Sven in a rented boat. They could not catch a thing. Ole said, "Let's go a bit furder downstream." So they did, and they caught many monstrous fish. They had their limit, so they went home. On the way home, Sven said, "I marked da spot right in da middle of da boat, Ole."

"You stupid," said Ole. "How do you know ve vill get da same boat next time!"

Ole is hiking in the mountains of Norway, and he slips on a wet rock and falls over the edge of a 500-foot cliff. He falls twenty feet and grabs hold of a bush that's growing out of a rock. There he is, hanging, looking into this deep fjord down below him—certain death—and his hands start to perspire. He starts to lose his grip on the bush, and he yells out, "Is anybody up there?"

And he hears a deep voice ring out in the fjord, "I'm here, Ole. It's the Lord. Have faith. Let go of that bush and I will save you."

Ole looks down, looks up, and says, "Is anyone else up there?"

So there was a big snowstorm and a snow emergency was declared. Ole had to park his car on the odd-numbered side of the street. Two days later, more snow, and he had to park it on the even-numbered side of the street. The next day, another snowstorm, another snow emergency, odd-numbered side of the street, and Ole said, "Heck, Lena, I'm tired of this. I'm gonna leave the dang car in the garage and if they want to tow it, let 'em tow it."

Ole: Hello? Funeral home?

Funeral home: Yes?

Ole: My wife, Lena, died.

Funeral home: Oh, I'm sorry to hear that. We'll send someone right away to pick up the body. Where do you live?

Ole: At the end of Eucalyptus Drive.

Funeral home: Can you spell that for me?

Ole: How 'bout if I drag her over to Oak Street and you pick her up dere?

Sven and Ole go to the beach. After a couple hours, Sven says, "This ain't no fun. How come the girls ain't friendly to me?"

Ole says, "Well, I tell you, Sven, maybe if you put a potato in your swim trunks that would help."

So Sven does, but he comes back to Ole later, and he says, "I tried what you told me with da potato, but it didn't help."

Ole says, "No, Sven—you're supposed to put da potato in da front."

Lena: I'd better warn you, my husband will be home in an hour.

Henrik: But I haven't done anything I shouldn't do.

Lena: I know, but if you're going to, you'd better hurry up.

"Sven, you should be more careful about pulling down your window shades. I saw you and Lena making love last night."

"Ha, the joke's on you, Ole! I wasn't home last night!"

Ole goes to the doctor and says, "Doc, I got two problems. First, I seen dat Bob Dole on TV talkin' about how Vigoro can help your sex life dere. So I been dissolvin' a tablespoon of Vigoro in half a glass of water an' drinkin' it before bed every night, but so far it ain't done me a bit of good."

And the doctor says, "Ole, that's supposed to be Viagra. Vigoro ain't no medicine, it's just a fertilizer."

And Ole says, "Oh, vell, dat explains da berries, den."

The county game warden dies, and Sven and Ole devise a plan that will hopefully land one of them in the position. They flip a coin, and Ole calls it. "You'd be callin' the mayor, Sven," he says. So Sven calls up the mayor and says, "Mayor, I hear the game warden died last night. If it's all right with you, I'd like to take his place."

The mayor replies, "It's all right with me if it's all right with the undertaker."

Sven and Ole went fishing and the fish were biting pretty good, and while they were reeling in the fish, Sven he fell out of the boat. And Ole he got his fish in the boat and got the hook out and then he dove in for Sven, and he brought him up and laid him in the boat and he give him mouth to mouth. And Ole he thinks, "Pew, that sure was bad coffee Sven drank this morning." And then he looks and he says, "Hey, Sven didn't have a snowmobile suit on when he fell out of the boat…I wonder who this is?"

Lena: Oh, Ole. I'm glad you got home. A burglar broke into the house last night while I was sleeping.

Ole: Did he get anything, Lena?

Lena: He sure did. But only because I thought it was you.

Ole: Well, guess what, Lena. I just bought a condominium.

Lena: Well, that's good, Ole. Now I can throw away my diagram.

Ole: When I die, I want to be buried at sea. Just because Lena keeps saying she's going to dance on my grave.

Sven: Well, that's a lovely family, Ole. Five boys. Looks like you got a boy every single time.

Ole: Oh, no, sometimes we didn't get anything.

Sven: Lena, I hear that Ole's father and mother were first cousins.

Lena: Ya. That's why he looks so much alike.

Sven: Working hard, Ole?

Ole: Nope. I'm fooling the boss. I'm carrying the same load of cement up and down the steps all day.

Lena: My two specialties are meatballs and peach pie.

Ole: I see. And which one is this?

Ole: Hey, Sven! Lookit here. I just bought a rare antique coin. More than two thousand years old. Look, it says 93 B.C. right on the front of it.

Lena: I'm so proud of my two boys. They became pilots. The other guys haul the cow manure out of the barn and my boys pile it.

So Ole and Lena were going to take a cruise to celebrate their 50th anniversary, and Lena said, "On the boat, I just want to make love like we did when we were young!" So Ole went to the drugstore and bought a bottle of pills for seasickness and a box of condoms. And the druggist said, "You know, if it makes you that sick, why do it?"

Ole was visiting the Vatican and went to see the Sistine Chapel. The tour guide told him that it took four years to paint the ceiling. Ole said, "Yeah, I used to have a landlord like that myself."

Sven: So, Ole, I hear that Ole Jr.'s gone to college.
   Ole: Yeah, that's right, Sven.
   Sven: So what do you think he'll be when he graduates?
   Ole: Probably about 35 or 40.

Ole was sitting in a coffeeshop in Hinckley when a man he recognized walked in, so he said, "Hey, Larson! Boy, look at you. When I knew you, you had a headful of hair, and now you're bald and you shaved off your moustache and you're wearing glasses."
   The guy replies, "I'm Benny Carlson—" and Ole says, "And you changed your name, too!"

Ole was dying. On his deathbed, he looked up and said, "Is my wife here?"

Lena replied, "Yes, Ole, I'm here, next to you."

So Ole asks, "Are my children here?"

"Yes, Daddy, we're all here," say the children.

"Are my other relatives also here?"

And they say, "Yes, we are all here."

Ole says, "Then why is the light on in the kitchen?"

Did you hear about the skeleton they found in Willmar last week?

Yeah, it was the winner of the 1965 Sons of Norway hide and seek contest.

One day, Sven and Ole were hunting and suddenly a man came running out of the bushes, yelling, "Don't shoot! Don't shoot! I'm not a deer!" Ole raised his gun and shot him dead.

Sven said, "Ole, why did you shoot that man? He said he wasn't a deer!"

Ole answered, "Oh! I thought he said he was a deer!"

Lena: Ole, how come you're sitting in the living room with no clothes on?

Ole: Well, nobody's going to come visit me so what does it matter?

Lena: But you got your hat on.

Ole: Well, you never know...

Sven: So, Ole, I see you burnt your ears pretty bad. What happened then?

Ole: Well, I was ironing a shirt, you know, and the telephone rang, and I put the iron to my ear.

Sven: Oh, for dumb. And what about the other?

Ole: Well, then I went to call the doctor…

Ole and Lena were celebrating their twenty-fifth anniversary. After the guests left, Lena looked at Ole and punched him real hard in the shoulder. "That's for twenty-five years of bad sex."

Ole thinks about it and then reaches over and punches Lena hard in the shoulder, "That's for knowing the difference!"

IOWA JOKES

Did you hear about the Iowans who went to the drive-in movie and hated it so much that they got rowdy and ripped up the seats?

Did you hear about the Iowa coyote?
    He chewed off three legs and was still caught in the trap.

Did you hear what happened to the Iowa ice hockey team?
    They drowned during spring training.

The Iowan walks into the hardware store to buy a chainsaw. He says, "I want one that will cut down about ten trees in an hour." So the clerk sells him one.
    The next day, the Iowan comes in all upset and says, "Hey, this chainsaw only cut down one little tree in one hour!" The clerk says, "Gee, let me take a look at it." He pulls on the starter rope, the saw starts up, and the Iowan says, "Hey, what's that noise?"

Why don't they take coffee breaks in Iowa?
    It takes too long to retrain them.

What do they call 100 John Deeres circling a McDonald's in Iowa?
    Prom night.

How do you make an Iowan's eyes light up?
    Stick a flashlight in his ear.

The Iowan checks into a hotel for the first time in his life and goes up to his room. Soon he calls the desk and says, "You've given me a room with no exit. How do I leave?"

The desk clerk says, "Sir, that's absurd. Have you looked for the door?"

The Iowan says, "Well, there's one door that leads to the bathroom. There's a second door that goes into the closet. And there's a door I haven't tried, but it has a 'Do Not Disturb' sign on it."

The Minnesota man and the Iowa man have just finished using the men's room and the Iowan stops to wash his hands. He says, "In Iowa, we're brought up to wash our hands after we pee." The Minnesotan says, "In Minnesota, we're brought up not to pee on our hands."

The Iowan was asked to use the word "fascinate" in a sentence.

He said, "My sister has a sweater with ten buttons, but her chest is so big she can only fasten eight."

Did you hear about the Iowa woman who went to the department store to return a scarf?

She claimed that it was too tight.

How do you know when an Iowan has been using your computer?

There are eraser marks on the screen.

The Iowan came to Minneapolis to see the sights and asked the hotel clerk about the time of meals. "Breakfast is served from seven to eleven, dinner from twelve to three, and supper from six to eight," explained the clerk. "Look here," inquired the Iowan in surprise, "when am I going to get time to see the city?"

Two Iowans were sitting in the doctor's waiting room. One of them was crying. The other Iowan asked, "Why are you crying?"

The first Iowan replied, "I came here for a blood test, and they had to cut my finger."

Upon hearing this, the second one started crying. The first one was astonished and asked the other, "Why are you crying?"

The second Iowan says, "I'm here for a urine test."

Did you hear about the Iowan who stayed up all night to see where the sun went?

It finally dawned on him.

Why do Iowans use birth-control pills?

So they'll know what day of the week it is.

And why do they stop using birth-control pills?

Because the pills keep falling out.

Why don't Iowans make Jell-O?

They can't figure out how to get two cups of water into those little bags.

Why don't Iowans eat pickles?
    They can't get their heads in the jar.

So this Iowan died and went to heaven. St. Peter said,
"Before I let you in, you have to pass a test."
    "Oh, no!" said the Iowan.
    St. Peter said, "Don't worry. This is easy. Just answer this
question: Who was God's son?"
    The Iowan thought. Finally, she said, "Andy!"
    St. Peter said, "Andy?"
    The Iowan said, "We sang it in church: 'Andy walks with
me, Andy talks with me, Andy tells me I am his own.'"

Why do Iowans hate to make chocolate chip cookies?
    It takes too long to peel the M&M's.

What about the Iowan who went to the library and
checked out a book called *How to Hug*?
    He got home and found out it was volume seven of the
encyclopedia.

On his first day at work, a recent University of Iowa
graduate was handed a broom by his new boss and told to
sweep the floor. He looked at the boss with disgust and
said, "Hey! I'm a graduate of the University of Iowa, you
know!"
    The manager took the broom back and said, "Really?
Sorry about that. Here, let me show you how it's done."

Why can't an Iowan dial 911?
    He can't find the eleven.

MINNESOTA JOKES

Why are most Iowa jokes so short?
   So Minnesotans can remember them.

The Vikings' placekicker tried to commit suicide after they lost to Atlanta.
   He got the rope around his neck, but he couldn't kick the bucket out from under him.

Did you hear that Denny Green wouldn't let the Vikings eat cereal?
   When they get close to a bowl, they choke.

If a Palestinian and a Minnesotan get married, what do they call their child?
   Yasir Yabetcha.

Guy #1: You know, once it got so cold in Minnesota…
   Guy #2: How cold did it get?
   Guy #1: So cold, I woke up in the morning and found these little chunks of ice in my bed, and when I warmed them up they went, pppppppppppppppp.

What did the Minnesotan say to the Pillsbury Doughboy?
   "Hey, man—nice tan."

Where do you find the trees in Minnesota?
   Between da twos and da fours.

A boy worked in the produce section of the supermarket. A man came in and asked to buy half a head of lettuce. The boy told him they only sold whole heads of lettuce, but the man was persistent. The boy said he'd go ask his manager what to do.

The boy walked into the back room and said, "There's some jerk out there who wants to buy only half a head of lettuce."

As he finished saying this he turned around to find the man standing right behind him, so he added, "And this gentleman wants to buy the other half."

The manager okayed the deal. Later the manager said to the boy, "You almost got yourself in a lot of trouble earlier, but I must say I was impressed with the way you got yourself out of it. You think on your feet, and we like that around here. Where are you from, son?"

The boy replied, "Minnesota, sir."

"Oh really? Why did you leave Minnesota?" asked the manager.

The boy replied, "They're all just whores and hockey players up there."

"My wife is from Minnesota," the manager said.

The boy replied, "Really!? What team did she play for?"

NORTH DAKOTA JOKES

Two North Dakotans are skydiving. One jumps out of the plane and pulls the cord—nothing happens. So he pulls the emergency cord—still nothing. The other one jumps out of the plane and yells, "Oh! So you wanna race, huh?"

Two North Dakotans go into a bar, and they buy drinks for everybody in the place. They're celebrating and whooping it up, slapping everybody on the back. So the bartender says, "What are you whooping it up for? What's the occasion?"

They say, "We just finished a jigsaw puzzle, and it only took us two months!"

The bartender says, "Two months! What's the big deal? It shouldn't take that long to do a jigsaw puzzle!"

"Oh yeah?" says one of the North Dakotans. "On the box it said two to four years!"

How is a divorce in North Dakota like a hurricane in Florida?

Either way, you lose the trailer.

The train for Chicago leaves at 1:15, the train for Duluth leaves at 1:30, and the train for Fargo leaves when the big hand is on the 9 and the little hand is on the 1.

What is a seven-course meal in North Dakota?

A hamburger and a six-pack.

AND A FEW JOKES BEYOND US

A Frenchman, a German, and a Jew are lost in the desert, wandering for hours. The Frenchman says, "I'm tired. I'm thirsty. I must have wine." The German says, "I'm tired. I'm thirsty. I must have beer." The Jew says, "I'm tired. I'm thirsty. I must have diabetes."

A mine owner advertised for new workers and three guys turned up—an Irishman, an Italian, and a Japanese. The owner tells the Irishman, "You'll be in charge of the mining." He tells the Italian, "You'll be in charge of the lift." He tells the Japanese, "You'll be in charge of making sure we have supplies." The next day the three men went into the mine, and at the end of the day one man was missing, the Japanese. They searched for him for hours. Just as they were about to give up, he jumped out from behind a rock yelling, "Supplies! Supplies!"

Son: Mama, I have da biggest feet in da third grade. Is dat becoss I'm Norvegian?
   Mom: No, it's because you're nineteen.

What do you call a Norwegian under a wheelbarrow?
   A mechanic.

What's the difference between a Norwegian and a canoe?
   A canoe will sometimes tip.

What do you call a Norwegian car?
   A Fjord.

Did you hear about the Norwegian who lost fifty dollars on the football game?

Twenty-five on the game, and twenty-five on the instant replay.

Did you hear about the Norwegian speed skater who won a gold medal in the winter Olympics?

He was so proud, he had it bronzed.

Did you hear about the Miss Norway Contest where the winner came in third?

I went into this Cajun/Norwegian restaurant. They served blackened toast.

How can you tell when you're talking to a Finnish extrovert?

He looks at *your* shoes.

Did you hear about the Finnish husband who loved his wife so much he almost told her?

A Texan was trying to impress a guy from Boston with an account of the heroism at the Alamo. He says, "I guess you don't have many heroes where you're from?"

The Bostonian replies, "Well, have you ever heard of Paul Revere?"

And the Texan says, "Paul Revere? Isn't he the guy who ran for help?"

Late one hot morning, two tourists driving through Louisiana saw on the map that the next logical stop for lunch would be at a town called Natchitoches. They wondered about the pronunciation, one favoring NATCH-ee-toe-cheese and the other saying it made more sense as Natch-eye-TOTT-chez. They stopped at a franchise burger place and went inside; a fresh-faced girl took their order. One said: "We need somebody local to settle an argument for us. Could you please pronounce where we are…very slowly?" The girl leaned over the counter so they could watch her lips and said as distinctly as she could, "Brrrrrrrr, grrrrrrr, Kiiiiinngg."

A Texan, a Russian, and a New Yorker went to a restaurant in London, and the waiter said, "Excuse me, but if you order the steak you might not get one, as there is a shortage." The Texan said, "What's a shortage?" The Russian said, "What's a steak?" The New Yorker said, "What's excuse me?"

The reason New Yorkers are depressed is because the light at the end of the tunnel is New Jersey.

Did you hear about the hurricane that hit New Jersey and inflicted $11 million worth of improvements?

What's the difference between a Yankee Stadium hotdog, and a Fenway Park hotdog?
 You can buy a Yankee Stadium hotdog in October.

New York is a place where all the girls are looking for husbands and all the husbands are looking for girls.

219

New York is a place where you spend more than you make, on things you don't need, to impress people you don't like.

New York is where you can get the best cheap meal and the lousiest expensive meal in the country.

In New York, if you don't have a shrink, you gotta be crazy.

Why does the Boston rowing team beat the New York rowing team?
    Because the Boston team has one guy yelling, and eight guys rowing.

The difference between the Upper West Side and the Upper East Side is that on the Upper East Side, the Salvation Army bands have a harp and a string section.

A tourist is heading for his car when he sees a guy breaking into his trunk. He yells, "Hey, this is my car!" The guy says, "OK, you take the radio and I'll take the tires."

Rules for driving in New York City:
    • Keep to the right on a one-way street.
    • Take the first parking space you see. There will not be another.
    • Don't get in the way of a car that needs extensive bodywork.
    • Always look both ways when running a red light.
    • Never signal a lane change. It only gives other drivers a chance to speed up and not let you in.
    • Making eye contact revokes your right of way.

Why are Yankee fans like laxatives?
  Because they irritate the crap out of you.

If you live in Green Bay, Wisconsin, how do you keep bears
out of your backyard?
  Put up goalposts.

A German tourist was driving 140 miles an hour in his
BMW, and the highway patrol pulled him over. The
patrolman said, "I'm going to have to search your car."
  "Okay, javohl," said the German. The patrolman looked
inside the trunk, and there was a piece of raw, bloody meat.
When he questioned the German, he said, "Oh ja, that is
mine spare veal!"

An old Irishman was coming home late one night from the
pub. As he passed the old graveyard, he thought of all his
friends in there, and then he saw a stone beside the road.
He thought, "The poor man, buried out here by the
highway. And he lived to the ripe old age of 145. A fine
man. Let's see, his name was Miles, from Dublin."

When the Irish say that St. Patrick chased the snakes out of
Ireland, what they don't tell you is that he was the only one
who SAW any snakes!

Did you hear about the Irish attempt on Mount Everest?
They ran out of scaffolding.

"Excuse me, Kate, may I come in? I've somethin' to tell ya."

"Of course you can come in, you're always welcome. But where's my husband?"

"That's what I'm here to be tellin' ya, Kate. There was an accident down at the Guinness brewery…"

"Oh, God, no!" cries Kate. "Please don't tell me…"

"I must, Kate. Your husband Patrick is dead and gone. I'm sorry."

Finally, she looked up. "How did it happen?"

"It was terrible, Kate. He fell into a vat of Guinness Stout and drowned."

"Oh, my dear Jesus! But you must tell me true, did he at least go quickly?"

"Well, no, Kate…no. Not really. Fact is, he got out three times to pee."

The difference between good ol' boys and rednecks is that good ol' boys may raise livestock, but rednecks get emotionally involved.

A Brit, a Frenchman and a Russian are viewing a painting of Adam and Eve frolicking in the Garden of Eden. The Brit said, "They look so calm. They must be British." The Frenchman said, "Nonsense. They're naked, and so beautiful. Clearly, these are French people." The Russian disagreed, "I don't think so. They have no clothes, no shelter, they have only an apple to eat, and they're being told this is paradise. They are Russian."

An American went to live in the Shetland Islands. He bought a house in the middle of nowhere and lived there for three months and saw no one. One day there was a knock on the door. He opened the door and there was a howling gale outside and there stood a six-foot-four Shetlander with a dirty old sweater and a huge beard and he said "I'm here to welcome you to the Shetland Islands."

"Hi! It's really nice to see you," the American said.

"I'm here to invite you to a party."

"I've been here for three months on my own, I haven't seen a soul," said the American. "I'd be delighted to come to a party."

"But I have to warn you, it will be a wild Shetland party," said the Shetlander. "There's going to be drinking."

"Well, I like a little drop of Scotch now and again. I can hold my own with the best of them for drinking" said the American.

"And there's going to be wild Shetland dancing."

"Well, when I was in college, I was considered very light on my feet."

"There's going to be a fight. There's always a fight"

"Well, actually, when I was in the military, I was the unit boxing champion, so I can hold my own."

"And then," said the Shetlander, "there's going to be sex. Wild Shetland sex."

"Well, I've been here for three months, and I haven't seen a soul. A little bit of that wouldn't be out of the question either. So, what should I wear?"

"Just you come as you are. It's just going to be you and me."

They've passed a law in Texas that says a woman has to wait to inherit her husband's estate until she's fourteen.

An Alaskan was on trial in Anchorage. The judge turned to him and asked, "Where were you on the night of October to April?"

The difference between comedy and tragedy in Russian drama is that in tragedy, everybody dies; but in the comedy, they die happy.

OLD PEOPLE JOKES

Old lady: Do you remember when we were first married and you used to take my hand and kiss me on the cheek and then you'd kind of nibble on my ear?

Old man: You bet. Let me go get my teeth.

Old lady: Do you remember if we ever had mutual orgasm?

Old man: Mutual orgasm? No, we always had Allstate.

Mildred was a ninety-three-year-old woman who was particularly despondent over the recent death of her husband, Earl. She decided to kill herself and join him in death. Thinking that it would be best to get it over with quickly, she took out Earl's old army pistol and made the decision to shoot herself in the heart, since it was so badly broken in the first place. Not wanting to miss this vital organ and become a vegetable and a burden to someone, she called her doctor's office to inquire just exactly where the heart would be. "On a woman," the doctor said, "your heart would be just below your left breast." Later that night, Mildred was admitted to the hospital with a bullet wound to her left knee.

An old man is sitting on a park bench, sobbing, and a young man walks by and asks him what's wrong. The old man says, "I'm married to a beautiful twenty-two-year-old woman." The young man says, "What's wrong with that?" And the old man says, "I forgot where I live!"

First old man: You want to go for a walk?
Second old man: Isn't it windy?
First old man: No, it's Thursday.
Second old man: Me, too. Let's go get a beer.

It was Mr. Ryan's funeral and the pallbearers were carrying the casket out from the church. When they bumped into a pillar, one of them heard a moan from inside the casket. They opened the casket and found that Mr. Ryan was still alive. God be praised. He lived for ten more years before he finally died. Another funeral was held for him and, as the pallbearers were carrying out the casket, Mrs. Ryan said, "Watch out for that pillar!"

The old lady walks up to the old man at the retirement home and says, "If you drop your pants, I'll bet I can tell your age." So, the man drops his pants, and she says, "You're eighty-three."
"You're right! How could you tell?"
"You told me yesterday."

Why do they give old men in the nursing home Viagra before they go to sleep?
To keep them from rolling out of bed.

My grandmother started walking five miles a day when she was sixty.
She's ninety-seven today, and we don't know where the hell she is.

The old man thought his wife was going deaf, so he came up behind her and said, "Can you hear me, sweetheart?" No reply. He came closer and said it again. No reply. He spoke right into her ear and said, "Can you hear me now, honey?"

His wife said, "For the third time, yes."

This old guy goes to the doctor for a checkup.

Doctor: You're in great shape for a sixty-year-old.

Guy: Who says I'm sixty years old?

Doctor: You're not sixty? How old are you?

Guy: I turn eighty next month.

Doctor: Gosh, eighty! Do you mind if I ask you at what age your father died?

Guy: Who says my father's dead?

Doctor: He's not dead?

Guy: Nope, he'll be 104 this year.

Doctor: With such a good family medical history your grandfather must have been pretty old when he died.

Guy: Who says my grandfather's dead?

Doctor: He's not dead?!

Guy: Nope, he'll be 129 this year, and he's getting married next week.

Doctor: Gee-whiz! Why at his age would he want to get married?

Guy: Who says he wants to?

A man is celebrating his ninetieth birthday at the nursing home, and his friends decide to surprise him. They wheel in a big birthday cake and out pops a beautiful young woman who says, "Hi, I can give you some super sex!" The old man says, "Well, I guess I'll take the soup."

227

An eighty-year-old couple is having problems remembering things, so they go to the doctor to get checked out. They describe for the doctor the problems they are each having with their memory. After checking the couple out, the doctor tells them that they are physically okay, but that they might want to start writing things down to help them remember. The couple thanks the doctor and leaves. Later that night while watching TV, the old man gets up from his chair. His wife asks, "Where are you going?" He replies, "To the kitchen." She asks him for a bowl of ice cream and he replies, "Sure."

She then asks him, "Don't you think you should write it down so you can remember?" He says, "No, I can remember that."

"Well," she then says, "I also would like some strawberries on top. You had better write that down 'cause I know you'll forget." He says, "I can remember that, you want a bowl of ice cream with strawberries."

"Well," she replies, "I also would like whipped cream on top. I know you will forget that, so you better write it down." With irritation in his voice, he says, "I don't need to write that down, I can remember that."

He fumes off into the kitchen. When he returns twenty minutes later he hands her a plate of bacon and eggs. She stares at the plate for a moment and says, "You forgot my toast."

Grandma, I ate all the peanuts in the candy dish.

That's okay. Since I lost my dentures, I can only suck the chocolate off them anyway.

228

Sitting on the side of the highway waiting to catch speeding drivers, a state police officer sees a car puttering along at twenty-two miles per hour. He thinks to himself, "This driver is just as dangerous as a speeder!" So he turns on his lights and pulls the driver over. Approaching the car, he notices that there are five old ladies—two in the front seat and three in the back—wide-eyed and white as ghosts.

The driver, confused, says to him, "Officer, I don't understand. I was doing exactly the speed limit! What seems to be the problem?"

"Ma'am," the officer replies, "you weren't speeding, but you should know that driving slower than the speed limit can also be a danger to other drivers."

"Slower than the speed limit? No sir, I was doing the speed limit exactly—twenty-two miles an hour!" the old woman proudly replies.

The officer explains to her that twenty-two was the route number, not the speed limit. A bit embarrassed, the woman grins and thanks the officer for pointing out the error.

"Before I let you go, ma'am, I have to ask: Is everyone in this car okay? These women seem awfully shaken, and they haven't muttered a single peep this whole time."

"Oh, they'll be all right in a minute, officer. We just got off Route 119."

My teeth are gone, my digestion's a mess, my joints ache, but at least my mind is still there, knock on wood. (KNOCKS) Who's there?

Man, that Mrs. Johnson. I got her husband all laid out in the casket in his black suit and she comes in and says she wants him buried in a blue suit.

Oh boy.

She insists that it has to be a blue suit.

What'd you do?

Well, luckily, we got this body shipped out from Chicago and it came dressed in a blue suit.

So you switched suits?

Naw. I just switched heads.

First Old Man: So, tell me, how does an eighty-two-year-old man like yourself persuade a twenty-one-year-old beauty to be your bride?

Second Old Man: Easy. I lied about my age. I told her I was ninety-seven.

Celebrity: It's great to be here with you wonderful folks here at the nursing home. Does anybody here know who I am? Huh?

Old Woman: No, but don't worry. Go down to the front desk and they'll tell you.

Old Woman: I can't believe it, doctor. Pregnant? It can't be. I'm seventy years old.

Doctor: I have your husband on the phone, ma'am. I know you'd like him to be the first to know.

Old Woman: Gimme that phone—Listen to me, you old goat, you've gone and knocked me up!

Old Man: And to whom am I speaking?

GENDER-RELATED JOKES

Marriage is nature's way of preventing people from fighting with strangers.

What do you call a man who's lost 75 percent of his intelligence?
    Divorced.

My wife is such a bad cook that the flies took up a collection to fix the screen door.

My wife is such a bad cook that last week *Gourmet* magazine tried to buy her subscription back.

Why do men like BMWs?
    They can spell it.

How many men does it take to change a toilet-paper roll?
    Who knows, it's never happened.

What do you call a man with half a brain?
    Gifted.

What's the difference between government bonds and men?
    Bonds mature.

Why is it so hard for women to find men who are sensitive, caring, and good looking?
    Because those men already have boyfriends.

Husband: I haven't spoken to my wife for eighteen months—I don't like to interrupt her.

Women like silent men; they think we're listening.

Did you know there are female hormones in beer?
    Female hormones in beer? Impossible.
    There are. You drink a lot of beer and you get fat, you talk too much and don't make sense, you cry, and you can't drive a car.

Waitress: So, what'll it be, mister?
    Customer: Tell you what. I want my eggs hard and burned around the edges, I want my bacon burnt to a crisp, and I want my toast blackened and hard. I want my coffee bitter, and when you bring me my food, I want you to yell at me.
    Waitress: What, are you crazy?
    Customer: No, I'm homesick.

Why are men like blenders?
    You need one, but you're not quite sure why.

Why are women's brains cheaper than men's brains?
    Because women's are used.

How do you get a man to do sit-ups?
    Put the remote control between his toes.

Do you know why women fake orgasm?
    Because men fake foreplay.

232

I've never understood why women love cats. Cats are independent, they don't listen, they don't come in when you call, they like to stay out all night, and when they do come home they expect to be fed and stroked and then left alone to sleep. Everything that women hate in men, they love in cats.

I want to buy a shotgun for my husband.
   Yes ma'am, does he know what gauge he wants?
   No, he doesn't even know I'm going to shoot him.

So, a husband and wife are in bed watching *Who Wants to be a Millionaire* and the husband says, "Would you like to make love?"
   The wife says, "No."
   The husband says, "Is that your final answer?"
   The wife says, "Yes."
   The husband says, "Then I'd like to call a friend."

If a man is in the forest, talking to himself, with no woman around, is he still wrong?

If a woman is in the forest, talking to herself, with no man around, is she still complaining?

One good thing about having a woman for president—we wouldn't have to pay her as much.

What's the fastest way to a man's heart?
   Through the chest wall with a sharp knife.

You and your husband don't seem to have an awful lot in common. Why did you get married?

I suppose it was the old business of "opposites attract." He wasn't pregnant and I was.

Scientists have discovered a new food that lowers the female sex drive: wedding cake.

Why do female black widow spiders kill the males after mating?

To stop the snoring before it starts.

I never knew what real happiness was until I got married—then it was too late.

Wife: If I died, would you marry again?
Husband: Yes, I would.
Wife: And would you let her come into my house?
Husband: Yes.
Wife: Would she sleep in my bed?
Husband: Probably, yes.
Wife: Would she use my golf clubs?
Husband: Definitely not.
Wife: Oh, why not?
Husband: Because she's left-handed.

Did you know that the shortest sentence in the English language is, "I am."
Really. What's the longest sentence?
"I do."

I decided that instead of getting married I'd just buy a dog.
    Why?
    Because after the first year, a dog is still excited to see you.

Very few things upset my wife and it makes me feel special to be one of them.

Men pass gas more often than women because women never close their mouths long enough to let the pressure build up.

A woman comes home shouting, "Honey, pack your bags! I won the lottery!"
    The husband exclaims, "Wow! That's great! Should I pack for the ocean, or for the mountains, or what?"
    And she says, "I don't care. Just get the hell out."

Why were men given larger brains than dogs?
    So they won't hump your leg at a cocktail party.

A male and female pigeon made a date to meet on the ledge outside the fiftieth floor of the Chrysler Building. The female was there on time, but the male arrived an hour late.
    "Where were you? I was worried sick."
    "It was such a nice day, I decided to walk."

A young lady came home from a date looking sad. She told her mother, "Jeff proposed to me an hour ago."

"Then why are you so sad?" her mother asked.

"Because he also told me he was an atheist. Mom, he doesn't even believe there's a hell!"

Her mother replied, "Marry him anyway. Between the two of us, we'll show him how wrong he is."

A man walked into a supermarket and bought a loaf of bread, a pint of milk, and a frozen dinner for one. The woman at the checkout said, "You're single, aren't you?"

The man said, "Yeah, how did you guess?"

She said, "Because you're ugly."

Why did God make man before woman?

You need a rough draft before you make the final copy.

A man exercises by sucking his stomach in every time he sees a beautiful woman.

Son: Dad! I got a part in the school play! I play the husband.

Dad: Too bad they didn't give you a speaking role.

A wife wakes up in the middle of the night and finds her husband sitting on the bed crying. She asks, "What's wrong?"

He says, "Remember when your daddy caught us in your room when you were sixteen and told me I'd have to marry you or he was gonna send me to jail for thirty years?"

She says, "Yeah, but why are you thinking about that?"

He says, "I'd be a free man today."

After twelve years in prison, a man finally escapes. When he gets home, filthy and exhausted, his wife says, "Where have you been? You escaped eight hours ago!"

An Aztec says to the Inca, "Hey Pocapopeptl, how long have you been wearing that brassiere?"

And the Inca says, "Ever since my wife discovered it in my saddlebag!"

A man took his wife to the livestock show and they looked at the champion breeding bulls. The wife said, "Look here. It says that this bull mated over 150 times last year. Isn't that something!"

And the husband replied, "Yes, but it wasn't all with the same cow."

And God created woman. And she was good. She had two arms, two legs, and three breasts. And God asked woman what she would like to have changed about herself, and she asked for her middle breast to be removed. And it was good. She stood with her third breast in her hand and asked God what should be done with the useless boob. And God created man.

Wife: Let's go out and have some fun tonight.

Husband: Okay, but if you get home before I do, leave the hall light on.

A man's idea of planning for the future means that he buys two cases of beer instead of one.

A woman was going through her husband's desk drawer and discovered three soybeans in an envelope containing thirty dollars in cash. So she asked him about it.

And the husband said, "Well, I have to confess. Over the years, I haven't been completely faithful to you. But every time I cheated, I put a soybean in the drawer to remind myself."

"So where did the thirty dollars come from?" she asked.

"Well, when soybeans hit ten dollars a bushel, I decided to sell."

Dying man: You know, honey, you've always been with me through all my troubles. Through all my bad times, you've been there. When I got fired, you were there. When my business went down the toilet, you were there. When I had the heart attack, you were there, and when we lost the house, and then when I got liver cancer, you were always by my side. You know something?

Woman: What?

Dying man: I think you're bad luck.

Wife: Do you love me?

Husband: Of course I love you. If I didn't love you, we wouldn't have all this damn furniture. I mean, maybe there's no chemistry left between us, but there's still archaeology.

Ma'am, I think your husband has had enough to drink. He just slid under the table.

No, my husband just walked in the door.

A woman sends her husband out to buy some escargot for a dinner party that night. Instead of going straight to the store, the husband decides to stop at the local bar. He has a few beers, and then some more, and pretty soon he looks at his watch and finds he's over an hour late for the dinner party. He dashes to the store, picks up the escargot, and frantically drives home. When he walks in the door he can hear his wife coming from the kitchen. So he takes the bag of snails and quickly throws them all over the floor. When his wife walks into the room, he says, "Come on guys, we're almost there!"

Why did Dorothy get lost in Oz?
  She had three men giving her directions.

My wife has been great. In just three years of marriage, she's gotten me to stop drinking and stop smoking, taught me how to dress well, how to enjoy music and painting and fine literature, how to cook gourmet meals, and how to have confidence in myself. So I'm getting a divorce. Frankly, she just isn't good enough for me.

"Honey, would you like a BMW for your birthday?"
  "No, I don't think so."
  "How about a mink coat?"
  "No thanks."
  "How about a diamond necklace?"
  "No. I want a divorce."
  "Oh. I wasn't planning on spending that much."

239

Mr. Johnson, I have reviewed this case carefully and I've decided to give your wife $800 a week alimony.

That's very generous, your honor. And believe me, I'll try to help out a little myself now and then.

Honey, am I the first man you ever made love with?

Why does everyone ask me that?

Sex is hereditary. If your parents didn't have it, chances are you won't either.

How do girls get minks?

The same way minks get minks.

Men are like fine wine. They all start out like grapes, and it's our job to stomp on them and keep them in the dark until they mature into something we'd like to have dinner with.

Why do women have smaller feet than men?

So they can stand closer to the sink.

The most difficult thing for a man after a divorce is learning how to express himself.

I wanted to be a flight attendant because it's a chance to meet men. When they're strapped down.

What would you do if you caught another woman with your husband?

Well, I guess I'd break her cane and send her back to whatever institution she escaped from.

Wife: You know, that young couple next door are so sweet. Every morning, when he leaves the house, he kisses her goodbye, and every evening when he comes homes, he brings her a dozen roses. Now, why can't you do that?

Husband: I don't even know her.

Can I have your number?

It's in the phone book.

But I don't even know your name.

That's in the phone book, too.

Haven't I seen you somewhere before?

Yes. And that's why I don't go back there.

Hey, gorgeous, where have you been all my life?

For most of it, I wasn't born yet.

Your body is like a temple.

Sorry, no services today.

I would go to the end of the world for you.

Yes, but would you stay there?

I want you to be the mother of my children.

How many you got?

Man: I have a magic watch that tells me you aren't wearing any underwear.

Woman: But I am wearing underwear.

Man: Well, it's about an hour fast. So how do you like your eggs in the morning?

Woman: Unfertilized.

The CIA was accepting applications for an assassin. They narrowed the finalists to two men and one woman, and they gave them the final test. They gave each of them a gun and brought the first man in and pointed to the big wooden door and said, "Right in there is your wife. Go in and kill her." The man dropped the gun. He said, "I can't do it." They brought in the second man and said, "Your wife is behind that door. Go kill her." The second man walked to the door and put his hand on the knob but he couldn't do it either. Finally, they brought in the woman and told her, "Behind that door is your husband. Go and kill him." So she went through the door and they heard the gun start firing, one shot after another for 13 shots. Then they heard screaming, crashing, and banging on the walls. Then everything was quiet. The door opened slowly, and the woman came out, wiping the sweat from her brow, and she said, "Some idiot loaded the gun with blanks. So I had to strangle him."

Three gents in a bar are discussing a female acquaintance who is trying without success to have a family. The first says, "I believe she is impregnable." The second says, "I think she is inconceivable." The third disagrees, saying, "You're both off the mark. She is obviously unbearable."

Honey, something's always bugged me about the children. I can't help noticing that out of our eight kids, Ben looks different from all the others. I know it's a terrible thing to ask, but does he have a different father?

Yes, it's true. He does.

Please tell me. Who is Ben's father?

You.

I almost fell in love with a psychic but she left me before we met.

Old Man: So how was your date with Edgar last night?

Old Woman: Well, I had to slap his face.

Old Man: He tried to go too far?

Old Woman: No, I thought he was dead.

I saw two houseflies in the kitchen today. Both females.

How did you know they were females?

They were on the phone.

Priest: I'm so sorry to hear of Jim's passing, Mary. My deepest condolences.

Widow: Oh thank you, Father.

Priest: It's a hard time.

Widow: Yes, Father. It is.

Priest: And did he have any last requests?

Widow: Yes, Father. He did.

Priest: And what was his last request, Mary?

Widow: Well, he asked me to please put the gun down.

Husband: Before I die, darling, I have to confess something to you.

Wife: I know all about it, darling. That's why I poisoned you.

Wife: If you had to do it all over again, would you still marry me?

Husband: I guess so. If I had to.

Why does an archeologist make a good husband?

Because the older you get, the more interested he is in you.

The wife smacks her husband upside the head. He says, "Hey! What was that for?"

"That's for the piece of paper in your pants pocket with the name Marylou on it."

He explains, "That's from two weeks ago. I went to the races, and Marylou was the name of one of the horses I bet on."

She hits him again. He says, "Now what was that for?"

"Your horse called on the phone today."

The secret of our marriage is that my wife worries about the little things, like what we should spend money on and what we should do on weekends, and I worry about the big things, like… energy policy and…Canada and… NATO.

My wife came home the other night and told me to take off her blouse. Then she told me to take off her skirt. Then she told me never to wear her clothes again.

The reason my wife never farts is that she never closes her mouth long enough for the pressure to build up.

My husband gives himself bubble baths by eating beans for dinner.

The only thing I have in common with my husband is that we were married on the same day.

A man and his wife weren't speaking to each other and one night the man left a note for her saying, "Please wake me at 5:00 a.m. I have to be at work for an early meeting." The next morning the man woke up at 9:00 a.m., and noticed a piece of paper by his pillow. It said, "This is your 5:00 a.m. wake up."

BLONDE JOKES

Employer: I see you left some blanks on your job application, ma'am. Hair color. I see you're a blonde.
  Blonde: Oh. Right.
  Employer: How old are you?
  Blonde: (counting quickly under her breath) 22.
  Employer: What is your name?
  Blonde: (under her breath) Happy birthday to you, happy birthday to you…happy birthday, dear—MANDY.

The blonde looked at the other blonde who was wearing a nametag and she said,
  "'Debbie'…that's cute. What did you name the other one?"

Why do so many blondes move to L.A.?
  It's easy to spell.

How does a blonde know if she's on her way home or on her way to work?
  She opens her lunch box to see if it's empty.

How do you keep a blonde occupied for hours?
  Write "Please turn over" on both sides of a piece of paper.

Why don't blondes breastfeed?
  Because it's so painful to boil your nipples.

A blonde decided to kidnap a kid so she went to the playground, grabbed a kid, and wrote a note saying, "I've kidnapped your kid. Tomorrow morning, put $10,000 in a paper bag and put it under the tree next to the slide on the playground. Signed, A Blonde." The blonde pinned the note to the kid's shirt and sent him home.

The next morning the blonde checked, and sure enough, a paper bag was sitting under the tree. The blonde opened up the bag and found the $10,000 with a note that said, "How could you do this to a fellow blonde?"

A blonde walks into the hair salon with a pair of headphones on. The stylist asks her to take them off for the haircut, so she does, and a moment later she faints. The stylist picks up the headphones and there's a little voice saying, "Breathe in…breathe out…in… out…in."

A blonde walks down the street and sees a banana peel ahead, and she says: "Here we go again."

A blonde wanted to buy personalized license plates but she couldn't afford them. So she changed her name to JKM345.

A blonde and her father are walking down a street when the father says, "Look, a dead bird."

And the blonde looks up and says, "Where?"

How do you sink a submarine full of blondes?
Knock on the hatch.

Did you hear about the blonde couple that were found frozen to death in their car at a drive-in movie theater?

They went to see "Closed for the Winter."

What is it called when a blonde blows in another blonde's ear?

Data transfer.

JOKES FROM THE NEWS

They had a Presidents' Day Sale at Macy's—all men's pants were half off.

They took a poll of American women, and they asked, "Would you have an affair with Bill Clinton?"
   Seventy percent said, "Never again!!"

The Pope met with President Clinton. The good news was that they agreed on 80 percent of what they discussed. The bad news was that they were discussing the Ten Commandments.

President Clinton looks up from his desk in the Oval Office to see one of his aides nervously approaching him. "What is it?" the President asks.
   "It's the abortion bill, Mr. President. What do you want to do about it?" the aide asks.
   "Just go ahead and pay it," responds the President.

We always knew you could get AIDS from sex, and now President Clinton has shown us you can get sex from aides.

Why did Monica Lewinsky have sex with the president in the Oval Office?
   Because she didn't have $50,000 for the Lincoln Bedroom.

Bill Clinton liked Monica Lewinsky's dress from the first time he spotted it.

Monica walks into her dry cleaning store and says to the clerk, who is hard of hearing, "I've got another dress for you to clean." The clerk replies, "I'm sorry, come again?" "No," says Monica. "This time it's mustard."

He never told Monica Lewinsky to lie. He told her to lie down.

You know why Bill Clinton is so reluctant to deal with this young Cuban boy in Miami?

It's because the last time he decided where to put a Cuban he was impeached.

Dan Quayle, Newt Gingrich, and Bill Clinton went to the Emerald City to see the Wizard of Oz. And Dan Quayle says, "I'm going to ask the wizard for a brain."

And Newt Gingrich says, "I'm going to ask him for a heart."

And Clinton says, "I wonder where Dorothy is?"

What do you call it when the Vice President plays the drums?

Algorithm.

"Run Hillary Run!" bumper stickers are selling like hotcakes in New York.

Democrats put them on their rear bumpers; Republicans put them on the front.

God decides it's time to have the world end. He calls in Bill Clinton, Boris Yeltsin, and Bill Gates. He tells them that the world is going to end in seven days. So Clinton goes to the American people, and Yeltsin goes to the Russian people, and they say, "We have some good news and some bad news. The good news is, there is a God. The bad news is, the end of the world is coming."

And Bill Gates goes back to Microsoft and says, "I have some good news and some even better news. The good news is, I'm one of the three most important people on earth, and the even better news is we don't have to fix Windows '95!"

What's the difference between God and Bill Gates?
God doesn't think he's Bill Gates.

If you see Bill Gates on a bicycle, should you swerve to hit him?
No. It might be your bicycle.

Why should Bill Gates be buried 100 feet deep?
Because deep down, he's a really good man.

After Bill Gates and his wife returned from their honeymoon, she said to him, "Now I know why you named it Microsoft!"

Bill Gates built a new house for himself and it's great, except that sometimes when you flush the toilet it won't stop. When that happens you need to exit the house, walk around the block, re-enter the house, and usually it's better.

A little boy and a little girl were talking on the playground, and the little boy said, "My daddy's an accountant. What does your daddy do for a living?"

She said, "My daddy's Bill Gates."

"Honest?"

"No, I didn't say that."

You know something? If Bill Gates had a nickel for every time Windows crashed…. Oh wait, he does.

A man gets to make a wish, and he wishes he could wake up in bed with three women. When he wakes up, there are Lorena Bobbit, Tonya Harding, and Hillary Clinton. And his penis is gone, his leg is broken, and he has no health insurance.

Did you hear about the new pill? It makes you feel good but has the side effect of making you dull. It's called Prosaic.

Did you hear that after she broke her leg, Picabo Street, the Olympic skier, donated money for a very special hospital wing?

It's going to be called the Picabo ICU.

Did you hear that Louise Woodward will shortly be taking over as manager of the Spice Girls?

The first thing she intends to do is drop Baby Spice.

This woman went to hear Patrick Buchanan give his stump speech. She thought it was okay but would have been better in the original German.

252

So the Republican was riding in his limousine when he saw all these poor people on their hands and knees eating grass by the roadside. He stopped and asked them why they were eating grass and they said, "Because we don't have any money for food."

He said, "Well, come along with me then. I'll take care of you. The grass at my house is almost half a foot high."

A man goes into a shop to buy a car radio, and the salesman says, "This is the latest model. It's a voice-activated car radio. You just tell it what you want to listen to and the station changes. No need to take your hands off the wheel."

So the man has it installed and takes off down the road. He says, "Classical!" and a public radio station comes on with a Mozart symphony. Then he says, "Country!" and a Garth Brooks song comes on, and he listens to that. Then a guy drives by really fast and cuts in front of him, so he yells, "Stupid!" and the radio changes to Rush Limbaugh.

What were George W. Bush's three hardest years?
Second Grade.

President Bush was sitting in the Oval Office when a young man walked in the door and said, "Hey, you turkey."

The President said, "Do you know who I am? I'm the President of the United States. You can't say that to me."

The young man said, "Do you know who I am?"

The President said, "No."

The young man said, "Good."

A speechwriter for President Bush felt unappreciated by the president and so when the President came to give his next speech, he looked at the teleprompter and it said:

"Some say that this war against Iraq is all about oil. It isn't, and I'll tell you why."

"Some say that a tax cut will lead to even worse federal deficits. It won't, and I'll tell you why."

"Some say that my policies favor the wealthy over the middle class. They don't, and I'll tell you why."

And then there was a blank space on the teleprompter. And then the words:

"Okay, George, you take it from here."

Why are there no Walmarts in Afghanistan?
Because they're all Targets.

SPORTING JOKES

A kid was ice fishing, but wasn't having much luck. He saw a guy across the way who was hauling in a bounty of fish, one after another. So the kid went over to the guy and said, "What are you doing to get all these fish? I'm just a few feet away from you, and I'm not catching anything."

The guy answered in a muffled voice, "Ee yer erms orm." The kid didn't understand, and the guy tried to speak again, "Ee yer erms orm." The kid still couldn't understand him, so the guy said, spitting off to the side, "Spfffff...I said...keep your worms warm!"

A man phones home from his office and tells his wife, "I have a chance of a lifetime to go fishing for a week, but I have to leave right away. So pack my clothes, my fishing equipment, and my blue silk pajamas. I'll be home in about an hour to pick them up." He goes home, grabs everything, and rushes off. He returns a week later and his wife asks if he had a good time. He says, "Oh yes, great! But you forgot to pack my blue pajamas!"

His wife smiles and says, "Oh no, I didn't. I put them in your tackle box!"

Two backpackers see a bear about to charge them. One backpacker takes off his hiking boots and puts on running shoes. His companion says, "You'll never outrun the bear—why are you putting those on?" The guy with the running shoes responds, "I don't have to outrun the bear. I just have to outrun you."

255

Two guys out hunting find a hole in the woods that's about three feet across but so deep that when they drop a small rock in it, they hear no sound. They drop a bigger rock in it, and still no sound. So they go looking for something larger, and they find a railroad tie. They haul it over to the hole, heave it in, and it disappears without a sound. Then a goat comes running up at about sixty miles an hour and dives head first into the hole. And there's still no sound. Nothing.

Suddenly a farmer appears from the woods and says, "Hey! You fellas seen my goat around here?" And they say, "Well, there was a goat just ran by here real fast and dove into this hole here."

"Naw," says the farmer, "that wasn't my goat—my goat was tied up to a railroad tie."

A guy takes his boy tiger hunting. They're creeping through the weeds and the man says, "Son, this hunt marks your passage into manhood. Do you have any questions?" And the boy says, "Yes, if the tiger kills you, how do I get home?"

Alaska's Department of Fish and Game is advising hikers, hunters, and fishermen to take extra precautions and be observant. They advise that outdoor enthusiasts wear bells on their clothing and carry pepper spray. They also recommend watching out for fresh signs of bear activity, and learning the difference between black bear and grizzly bear dung: Black bear dung is smaller and contains lots of berries and squirrel fur. Grizzly bear dung has little bells in it and smells like pepper spray.

A woman went on vacation with her husband to a fishing resort. While he was taking a nap, she took the boat out so she could sunbathe. She anchored in the bay, and along came the sheriff in his boat and said, "Ma'am, there's no fishing here. I'm going to have to take you in."

She said, "But officer, I'm not fishing."

"But you have all the equipment, ma'am. I'll have to take you in."

At which point she said, "If you do that, I will charge you with rape."

"But I didn't even touch you," said the sheriff.

"Yes, that's true…but you have all the equipment."

Five doctors went duck hunting one day: a GP, a pediatrician, a psychiatrist, a surgeon, and a pathologist. After a while a bird came winging overhead. The GP raised his shotgun but didn't shoot because he wasn't sure if it was a duck or not. The pediatrician also raised his gun, but then he wasn't sure if it was a male or female duck, so he didn't shoot. The psychiatrist raised his gun and then thought, "I know that's a duck, but does the duck know it's a duck?" The surgeon was the only one who shot. BOOM!! He blew it away. Then he turned to the pathologist and said, "Go see if that was a duck."

First Football player: Hey, Tiny. Gimme the answer to that third one on page two. The fill in the blank, Old MacDonald had a what?

Second Football Player: Farm, you dummy.

First Football Player: Oh, right. Farm. How do you spell it?

Second Football Player: E-I-E-I-O.

A huge college freshman decided to try out for the football team. "Can you tackle?" asked the coach.

"Watch this," said the freshman, who proceeded to run smack into a telephone pole, and knocked it completely over.

"Wow," said the coach. "I'm impressed. Can you run?"

"Of course I can run," said the freshman. He was off like a shot, and in just over nine seconds, ran a hundred-yard dash.

"Great!" enthused the coach. "But can you pass a football?"

The freshman hesitated for a few seconds. "Well, sir," he said, "if I can swallow it, I can probably pass it."

A Scotsman went to a baseball game and enjoyed it, but when one batter got a walk and tossed the bat aside and strolled to first base, the Scotsman stood up and yelled, "Rrrrun, man! Rrrrun!" The fan next to him said, "He doesn't have to run, he's got four balls." And the Scotsman yelled, "Walk with pr-r-ride man! Walk with pr-r-ride!!!!"

Why was the team called a Cinderella team?

They kept running away from the ball.

Our team finished in last place because our batters never got to hit against our pitchers.

Our shortstop's having such a terrible season, he tried to kill himself the other day by jumping in front of a bus, but it went right through his legs.

Baseball is 90 percent mental. The other half is physical.

A Little League team had just been whipped, and the coach told them, "Boys, don't get down on yourselves. You did your best and you shouldn't take the loss personally. Keep your chins up. Your parents are just as proud of you boys as the parents of the girls' team that beat you."

Stevie Wonder and Tiger Woods were talking and Stevie said, "Tiger, I've been having trouble with my putting."
   Tiger said, "You play golf? But you're blind."
   Stevie said, "I know, but I just have my caddy put a beeper in the hole and I do pretty well. In fact, I'm usually under par."
   Tiger said, "Hey, we should play a round sometime."
   Stevie said, "Sure. Anytime. Pick a night."

A golfer was sitting in the clubhouse after playing a round. He looked upset, so his friend went over and asked what was wrong. The golfer said, "It was terrible. On the 16th hole I sliced one out onto the freeway and it went through the windshield of a bus, and there was a horrible accident. The bus went out of control and hit a car head-on. There were dead people all over the place."
   His friend said, "That's awful. What did you do?"
   "Well, I closed up my stance and shortened my backswing a little."

A guy takes a gorilla out golfing. They come up to the first tee, and the gorilla asks, "What am I supposed to do?" The guy says, "You see that little round green spot about 400 yards from here? You're supposed to hit the ball onto that." So the gorilla hauls off and whacks the ball, and it goes screaming down the fairway and lands on the green. The man drives his ball and it goes about 150 yards, and he hits an iron shot and a second iron shot and finally lands on the green, the gorilla following along behind him. They come to the green, and the gorilla says, "What do I do now?" The man says, "Now you hit it into that cup." The gorilla says, "Why didn't you tell me that back there?"

A young man was playing this hole with a senior citizen. Just as the older man was about ready to hit his tee shot he noticed a funeral procession approaching. He took off his hat, put it over his heart, and stood silently and watched the procession go by until it disappeared.

The younger man said, "That's really nice of you. Do you always do that when a funeral goes by?"

"No," said the senior citizen, "not usually, but it's the least I could do in this case. I was married to the woman for forty years!"

LAST-BUT-NOT-LEAST JOKES

"Would you like a cup of coffee?"

"No, thanks. When I drink coffee I can't sleep."

"Huhh. In my case it's the other way around. When I sleep, I can't drink coffee."

"Hello? Is this the fire department?"

"Yes."

"Listen, my house is on fire! You've got to come right away! It's terrible!"

"Okay, how do we get to your house?"

"You don't have those big red trucks anymore?"

A horse is tied up at a hitching post. A little dog comes along and starts playing around the horse. The horse gets annoyed and starts pawing the ground.

The dog looks up and asks, "What are you doing that for?"

The horse looks down and says, "Well, I'll be damned, a talking dog."

Mr. Johnson, I want to speak with you about your son. I discovered him playing doctor with my daughter!

Well, it's only natural for children that age to explore their sexuality in the form of play.

Sexuality?! He took out her appendix!

Two cows are lying in a field. One of them says to the other, "So, what do you think about this mad cow disease?"

The other says, "What do I care? I'm a helicopter."

261

Miss Francis, I ain't got no crayons.

Young man, you mean, I don't have any crayons. You don't have any crayons. We don't have any crayons. They don't have any crayons. Do you see what I'm getting at?

I think so. What happened to all the crayons?

I was driving to work the other day when I hit a pig. I was just gonna drive away when I thought better of it and called the police to tell them.

The dispatcher said, "Thanks for calling us, but don't you go anywhere. It's illegal to hit livestock in this state. That's a $300 fine."

So I hung up, got in the car, and drove off. When I got to work there was a cop waiting for me. He gave me a ticket for $300. When I asked him how he found me he said, "The pig squealed."

I was walking down the street and saw two guys trying to steal an old lady's handbag. She was putting up quite a fight, and I didn't know if I should get involved or not. Finally I decided to help, and it didn't take the three of us very long to get it away from her.

Two penguins are standing on an iceberg. One penguin says to the other, "You look like you're wearing a tuxedo."

The other penguin replies, "Who says I'm not?"

The baby snake says to the mommy snake, "Mommy, are we poisonous?"

The mommy snake says, "Why do you ask?"

And the baby snake says, "Because I just bit my tongue."

A girl brought her new boyfriend home to meet her parents and they were horrified by his greasy hair, tattoos, dirty language, and air of hostility. After he left, the mother said, "Dear, he doesn't seem like a very nice person." And the daughter said, "Mother, if he wasn't a nice person, why would he be doing 500 hours of community service?"

One night, a caveman comes running into his cave and says, "Whew! There was a tiger chasing me all the way across the savannah!"
His wife says, "Why?"
The caveman says, "I didn't stop to ask!"

One day a guy answers his door and finds a snail at his doorstep. The guy picks it up and tosses it into the garden. Two years later, he hears a knock on his door. He opens the door and finds the same snail. And the snail says, "Hey, what was that all about?"

In the middle of a show, a guy stands up and yells at the ventriloquist, "Hey! You've been making enough jokes about us Polish people! Cut it out!"
The ventriloquist says, "Take it easy. They're only jokes!"
And the guy says, "I'm not talking to you. I'm talking to that little guy sitting on your knee!"

Hotel Clerk: Would you like the sixty dollar room or the eighty dollar room?
Guest: What's the difference?
Clerk: The eighty dollar room has free TV.

Two ladies are sitting next to each other on the plane, one from the north and one from the south. The lady from the south turns to the lady from the north and says, "Where y'all from?" The lady from the north says, "We are from a place where we do not end our sentences with prepositions."

The flight continues for an hour or so, and finally the lady from the south says, "So where y'all from, bitch?"

This man buys a pet parrot and brings him home. But the parrot starts cursing him and using terrible language and insulting his wife, so finally the man picks up the parrot and throws him in the freezer to teach him a lesson.

He hears the parrot squawking and screaming in there for a while, and then all of a sudden the parrot is quiet. So the man opens the freezer door, and the parrot walks out, looks up at him, and says, "I apologize for offending you, and I humbly ask your forgiveness."

The man says, "Well, thank you, I forgive you. "

And the parrot says, "If you don't mind my asking, what did the chicken do?"

When I was kid, we were so poor that when my little brother broke his arm we had to take him out to the airport for x-rays.

We were so poor, my dad would eat Cheerios with a fork so he could pass the milk around the table.

We were so poor, we'd lick stamps for dinner.

We were so poor, we didn't even use the "o" and "r."

A dog owner takes his sick dog to the vet. The vet examines the dog and pronounces it terminally ill. The pet owner requests a second opinion. So the vet brings his own kitten in, and the kitten examines the sick dog and shakes his head. The pet owner requests another opinion. This time the vet brings in his Labrador retriever, who jumps up on the examining table with the sick dog, sniffs and licks it, and then also shakes his head. The pet owner, now convinced, asks how much he owes the doctor. The doctor says he owes $650. The pet owner, surprised, asks why the bill is so high. The doctor replies that the exam was only $50; the additional $600 was for the cat scan and the lab test.

My father decided that I should learn how to swim. We went to one of the lakes in the area, and my father put a boat in the water. He rowed me out a little way from shore and threw me overboard. I swam back to shore. He took me out farther and threw me overboard again. Again, I swam back to shore. He took me out still farther, to the deepest part of the lake, and threw me overboard once more. I swam back to shore again. That's how I learned to swim. Actually, learning to swim wasn't the hard part—it was getting out of that burlap bag.

We went to this wonderful restaurant today and I can't remember the name of it. What's that flower with the sharp thorns that can be red, white, or pink?
Rose?
Yeah. Hey, Rose, what's the name of that restaurant?

So I came into town around midnight, but there was only one hotel and the clerk said every room was taken.

So what did you do?

I begged. I got down on my knees. I said, "You've got to have a room. Anything. Please."

And?

Finally, she said, "Well, I do have a double room with only one occupant, and probably he wouldn't mind splitting the cost, but to tell you the truth, he snores so loud that people down the hall complain about it. You won't get a minute of sleep."

So what'd you do?

I took the room.

How'd you sleep?

No problem.

Didn't the other guy snore?

No. I got dressed for bed, went over, gave him a kiss on the cheek, said, "Goodnight, beautiful," and he sat up all night watching me.

Sad man: Lady, I wonder if you wouldn't give a few bucks to help out a poor family here in the neighborhood. The father is dead, the mother is too sick to work, the nine children are hungry, and they're about to be thrown out into the street unless they can pay their rent.

Woman: How terrible! Are you a friend of theirs?

Sad man: I'm their landlord.

A visitor to a dude ranch is walking around the corral one day and sees one of the older hands feeding the horses. He walks over and strikes up a conversation.

"How long have you worked here?" he asks.

"Twenty-five years," the ranch hand says.

"Ever had any accidents?"

"Nope," says the ranch hand, "none at all."

"Really?" says the visitor. "Twenty-five years, and not a single problem?"

"Well," says the ranch hand, "I did get bit on the hand by a horse once."

"Well, isn't that an accident?" asks the visitor.

"Nope," says the ranch hand. "He bit me on purpose."

Ticket seller: Excuse me, ma'am. Your son is traveling on a child's ticket?! How old is he?

Mother: He's four years old.

Ticket seller: He looks at least twelve to me.

Mother: Can I help it if he worries?

Diner: I'd like a hamburger. But without onions please.

Cook: I'm sorry, we're all out of onions. I'll have to make it without tomatoes instead.

Waitress: What can I get you?

Customer: Couple of eggs.

Waitress: How would you like those eggs cooked?

Customer: Yeah, I would.

A group from Chicago spent a weekend gambling in Las Vegas. One of the men on that trip won $100,000. He didn't want anyone to know about it, so he decided not to return with the others. He took a later plane home, arriving back at 3 a.m. He immediately went out to the backyard of his house, dug a hole, and planted the money in it. The following morning he walked outside and found only an empty hole. He noticed footsteps leading from the hole to the house next door, which was owned by a deaf-mute. On the same street lived a professor who understood sign language and was a friend of the deaf man. Grabbing his pistol, the enraged man went to awaken the professor, and he dragged him over to the deaf man's house.

"You tell this guy that if he doesn't give me back my $100,000, I'm going to kill him!" he screamed at the professor. The professor conveyed the message to his friend, and his friend replied in sign language, "I hid it in my backyard, underneath the cherry tree."

The professor turned to the man with the gun and said, "He's not going to tell you. He said he'd rather die first."

My computer has a virus called the PBS virus. Every hour it freezes up and asks for money.

Did you hear about the robbery at the public radio station?
   The thieves got away with $25,000 in pledges.

A nearsighted whale was following the submarine. Every time it shot a torpedo, the whale passed out cigars.

A man was walking down the street with two suitcases when a stranger came up and asked, "Have you got the time?"

The man put down the suitcases, looked at his wristwatch, and said, "It's exactly five forty-six and fifty-point-six seconds, and the barometric pressure is 30.06 and rising, and if you'd like to see where we are by satellite positioning, I can show you that, too, or get onto the Internet, check your e-mail, make a long-distance call, or send a fax. It's also a pager, it plays recorded books, and it receives FM."

The stranger said, "That's amazing. I've got to have that watch. I'll pay you."

The guy said, "Oh, no, it's not ready for sale yet. I'm the inventor. I'm still working out the bugs."

The stranger offered him ten thousand, fifteen, twenty—finally the guy sold it for twenty-five thousand. He took the watch off his wrist, and the stranger walked away with it. The guy held up the suitcases and called, "Don't you want the batteries?"

Man: I hate this modern art. What a piece of crap that is.

Woman: No, that's a Picasso.

Man: What about this one with all these crazy squiggles?

Woman: That's a Kandinsky.

Man: Okay, how about this one where the guy's got a pencil neck, his nose is upside down, and his eyes are on the same side of his head?

Woman: That's a mirror.

Painter: What's your opinion of my painting?
    Critic: It's worthless.
    Painter: I know, but I'd like to hear it anyway.

I was having an asthma attack when I got an obscene phone call and after a couple minutes the guy said, "Wait. Did I call you or did you call me?"

Hey, Bob, remember when you and I went fishing up north nine months ago and the car broke down in that thunderstorm and we wound up spending the night at that farm owned by that gorgeous widow—you remember?
    Yeah.
    You remember the gorgeous widow?
    Yeah.
    And she had that big fabulous house and we slept in the guest wing and she was over in her wing and the next morning we got in our car and headed north and went fishing—you remember?
    Yeah.
    Well, nine months later, I get a letter from her attorney.
    Oh?
    Did you happen to get up in the middle of the night and go pay her a visit?
    I did. Yes.
    And did you happen to use my name instead of telling her your name?
    I'm sorry. I did. Why do you ask?
    She just died and left me everything.

You lied to me. You told me your father was dead, when in fact he's been in prison all these years.

Well, I don't call that living.

And he shot a priest.

It was a white collar crime.

I've got a dining room set that goes back to Louis the Fourteenth. That is, unless I pay Louis by the thirteenth.

A businessman in New York called his mother on Long Island. "Mom, it's me."

"Don't worry about not calling. If I had a stroke, probably it wouldn't be that bad."

"I'm sorry."

"Don't worry about not visiting me. If I were on the floor I could probably drag myself over to the phone and call for help."

"Mom, I've been terribly busy. I'm awfully sorry. But we're coming this weekend, the whole family. Me and Doris and the kids."

"Doris?"

"My wife, Doris."

"Your wife's name is Hannah!"

"Is this 516-555-9312?"

"9313."

"Oh, I'm terribly sorry, Madam."

"You mean you're not coming?"

Sadie, I–I tink I svallowed a bone.
  Are you choking, Hyman?
  No, I'm serious!

Woman running for garbage truck: Am I too late for the garbage?
  Garbage man: No, no. Hop right in.